S0-BLX-811

GOING THE DISTANCE

by

NADINE A. WOOLEY

Photographs by

Kristin Finnegan
Tony Capone
Bud Clark
Bill Blanchard
Terry Crawford
Yukihiko Yamaoki

Designer and Project Manager ■ Judith Ann Rose
Color House ■ Wy'east Color Inc.
Printer ■ Irwin-Hodson
Bindery ■ Lincoln & Allen

Published by the Friends of the Portland Marathon, Portland, Oregon

International Standard Book Number 0-9626697-0-9
Library of Congress Catalogue Card Number 90-83433

Cover photo by Kristin Finnegan

This book is dedicated to Les Smith.

TABLE OF CONTENTS

CHARTS & MAPS

Acknowledgments

The idea of writing this book came to me in the winter of 1988 as I contemplated what to do for my husband's upcoming fiftieth birthday. But as the idea unveiled itself in the spring of 1989, I realized that my intentions were as self-serving as they were selfless.

I had always wanted to write and publish a book and I loved running marathons. A diagnosis of Multiple Sclerosis in the summer of 1988 explained to me why training for and running marathons had become such a chore. I knew that eventually I would not run marathons, but I still wanted to be involved with the sport. Being married to the race director of the Portland Marathon, wanting to be active in the runner's world, and believing I had the talent and wherewithal to put together a book about the Portland Marathon encouraged me to begin.

Once my idea was well-hatched, I set out to get the support of my best friend and running partner, Julie Neupert—a businesswoman and a runner, for whom I have a great deal of respect. She listened. She raised question after question and finally she promised me her moral support.

My first goal was to surround myself with people in the business of designing and publishing books. Kris McIvor, editor of the *Winged* M and the only person I knew in the publishing industry, advised me to contact Judith Rose. Judith is well-known for *Timberline Lodge: A Love Story*. Her résumé and background convinced me she was the right one for the job. She became my Project Manager, publishing consultant, designer, and self-appointed best friend. Judith turned my idea into a reality. She kept me focused on the goal. She advised me in the world of book writing and publishing. She worked with everyone involved with this project. She buffered me from problems that would interfere with the time I needed to write. Without Judith, this book would never have gotten off the ground floor.

Judith introduced me to Catherine Gleason. Catherine is a wonderful editor. She is also a writer by profession and qualified, through the work of her trade, to be a writer's psychologist.

Writers seem to be plagued with afflictions that stop the creative flow, that cause mental lapses which make it impossible to retrieve ideas. Catherine was familiar with the symptoms, and I had many. She would call with words of encouragement. She would come to my home to pick up material, and I would explain that only part or none was completed because I had been brain dead for a week. She would not scold. She would offer a writer's remedy and be off. Her simple retreat would ignite the power in me to write. I could not disappoint Catherine.

For all her understanding, I thank her. She taught me to write better. She retaught me rules of grammar that I had learned in school and had long since forgotten. She forgave me when I kept making the same mistakes. I thank her for handling me with TLC and for being such a good teacher. Catherine is also a member of my small group of self-appointed best friends.

Before the tedious task of documenting this Marathon began, I had to contact members of the running community, specifically the Portland Marathon Committee, to find the answers to many questions and to locate pictures. The first to be contacted and offer support were Sherry Swain, Melinda Pyrch, and Peter Denes. They were all very helpful, each and every time I or Judith called, looking for pictures. Melinda, Sherry and Sheila Eadie (my editorial secretary and also my husband's legal secretary) helped Judith and me with the great picture caper. We pursued my husband's hundreds of Marathon pictures until we finally located them all. We stole them from his office, swiped them from his private shop, and contacted his contacts until we felt we had captured all the pictures we could. My thanks go to them.

Particular thanks go to Sherry Swain, who has given untold hours to the project, and helped to produce a prototype, and to Sheila Eadie, always on call to type, transcribe, engage in espionage, and help in any way possible. Uncomplaining, Sheila deciphered the manuscript and always gave back beautiful copy. Helping to create the prototype was Kate Peterson Victor. Kate worked with Judith to format and keyboard the manuscript for typesetting. For her last minute help with typesetting and layout, thanks to Anne Bothner-By .

Companies and individuals who have worked with Les professionally for years also participated in this great enterprise: Flashback Photography's Joe Hawes; Tony Capone, photographer; Clive Davies, artist; Luci Chiotti, graphic designer; the Gann Clan at Gann Publishing; T.J. McDonald at Irwin-Hodson Company; Dennis and Judy Ikenberry of Computerized Race-Results; and the entire Portland Marathon Race Committee.

A special thanks goes to Sheila Owings and Pat Holly for taking time with me on the phone while I read them the copy and waited for their changes. And a very special thanks goes to Patti Finke, who also spent hours on the phone with me listening to me belabor this project. Patti was always helpful and encouraging, as were Bob Williams, Hugh Mount, and Rebecca King.

There is also a very dear friend who has stood by me through the years in good and bad times. I described my idea to this friend and received wholehearted support. This support was both moral and financial. A very special thanks goes to this anonymous angel who helped get this project off to a flying start and who wishes to remain unknown.

And, of course, if it weren't for past race directors, there would be no present race. Ken Weidkamp, Bill Gorman, Leo Sherry, Brent Janes, and Kurt Hartung all willingly gave interviews to help me recreate the glorious history of the Portland Marathon. Les Smith, current race director, at first gave unknowingly of his expertise. Later, he gave even more information. All these men deserve thanks not only for this project, but for all they have given the running community and the City of Portland.

This book could not have been written without the support of my daughter, Ann Marie. She was a mere seven years when I began and now is the ripe old age of eight and a half. She has helped mom through the most trying times and is the best secret-keeper in the world.

Photography Acknowledgments

Tony Capone could take pictures of the Portland Marathon blindfolded. Piloting his motorcycle with aplomb, Tony has documented the Marathon since 1982.

He is the Marathon's official photographer (he is joined on race day by Mayor Bud Clark who also has official duties), and his dramatic black and white photographs have captured thousands of runners and have appeared in all Portland Marathon publications. Tony's black and white pictures form the running border of this book. A special thanks goes to Tony for his pictorial contributions.

Portland photographer Kristin Finnegan was smuggled onto the 1989 Marathon course with her gear and chauffeur-driven motorcycle to document the run and create a photographic surprise for Les Smith. A special thanks to her for dynamic photographs and hard work.

Joining photographers on the course and giving his special attention to the Five-Mile Mayor's Walk, his Honor, Bud Clark, has photographed walkers since the Mayor's Walk began in 1986. His energetic presence is a welcome addition to the Marathon.

Other contributing photographers are a very dedicated and talented Bill Blanchard, Terry Crawford, and Yukihiko Yamaoki.

ROMANCING THE MARATHON

A Prologue

"For every runner who tours the world running marathons, there are thousands who run to hear the leaves and listen to the rain . . ."

Dr. George Sheehan
Running doctor and writer

The marathon is a romance for the runner no matter how difficult, exhausting, or time-consuming. It is as romantic as that first kiss. It begins with love, moves into engagement, and ends with the commitment demanded by marriage, the feeling of joy that a truly challenging and successful marriage brings. Running the marathon has a golden glow that began twenty-five hundred years ago.

Once the runner has decided to run a marathon he enters a training period that by most standards is grueling. For the beginning runner, this may be a nine-month ordeal, like being pregnant and giving birth. But for the person who continues, the romance of running and preparing for a marathon fills and transforms his life.

The runner gets up in the morning, crawls out of bed, pulls on his running clothes (some runners have been known to sleep in their running gear), and heads out into the great outdoors, which may be city streets or a rural country road.

In the dead of winter, morning is quiet. The runner owns the road. If headlights move out of the darkness, his reflector vest glows. If there's ice on the road, he hears it crackling under his feet, giving him a running rhythm. If there's snow, the quiet grows even greater. The marathoner is no fair-weather friend. Like the mailman, neither rain, sleet, nor snow keeps him off the road.

The marathoner is the first to greet the spring. The light comes earlier. The birds begin to sing. He is wearing lighter clothes, and the air, especially if he runs early in the morning, is clear. In Portland, the mountains become visible. The sun lights up the sky behind Mt. Hood. He runs and watches the season unfold. Buds burst. Trees blossom. Walkers and joggers and short-distance runners appear.

By summer, the marathoner is rising earlier to avoid the heat, unless he belongs to that school of afternoon runners that likes to run with the sweat dripping down. New fragrances emerge. The air is thicker. He can smell green growth and dust. By now he is running at night as well, doing a track workout

■ Romance often blossoms at the Marathon. Britt Nelson and Chris Hardman met at the Post-race Party after the 1984 race and tied the knot fourteen months later. Fellow runner Dick Busby was best man.

■ Especially after a marathon, runners talk incessantly about running, while their

"widows" wait, unnoticed, in the background. If someone stripped and dashed stark naked through this crowd, the marathoners would go right on talking. . . about running.

■When asked why she left, a divorcee answered, "Because it was easier to move than to find storage space for

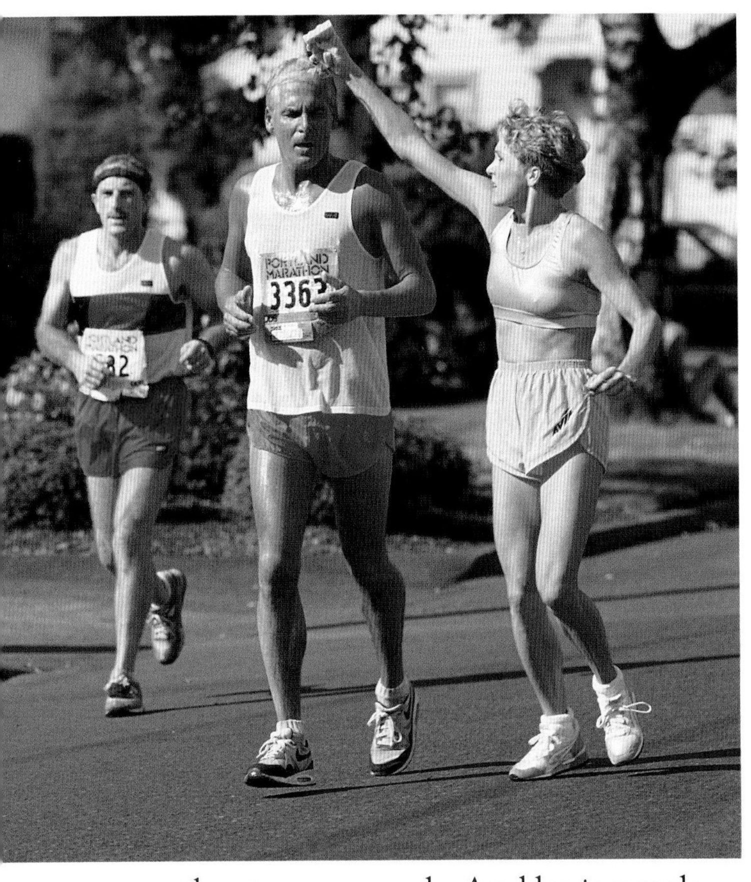

A marathoner receives a cool squeeze.

at least once a week. And he is watching the days slip toward autumn and waiting for that golden Sunday to draw near. For the Portland marathoner, autumn brings his work to fruition in a special harvest.

This kind of training, which may entail running sixty-five miles a week, is possible only because the marathoner loves what he or she is doing. The marathoner is a romantic, but the romance is only possible because of this deep commitment, the kind of commitment a man and woman make to a marriage if they want it to succeed.

This commitment encompasses many things. It includes taking care of your body, treating it properly, and giving it the right fuel. It means going out and running for miles even when you don't feel like it. It means being willing to learn from your body. In the same way that you have to be open-minded in a marriage, you have to be open-minded about listening to your body so that you don't strain or injure it. Marathoning is a discipline that contributes to your family life, as long as you're careful to weave it into the fabric of life at home. It's especially wonderful to share the marathon commitment with someone you love.

It was while running the Los Angeles Marathon that I met my marathon man. A mutual friend had introduced us several years earlier, during a 10K run in downtown Portland. In L.A., surrounded

hundreds of old running shoes, shirts, and shorts."

■**Dave and Sam first met at the packet stuffing party, preparing goody bags.**

The upshot was a dinner date. They have since become Dave and Sam Eddy.

■"Running makes you a better person," says Fred Lebow, Race

by thousands of runners, I noticed a man ahead of me whose quirky run looked familiar. I worked my way through throngs of runners and, although I couldn't remember his name, asked him if I could run with him.

We ran the entire marathon together, told each other our life stories, and stopped at mile twenty-one at a phone booth to call Hugh Mount, the mutual friend who had introduced us. Five months later, we were married and have been running marathons together ever since. We celebrated our honeymoon by running the Honolulu Marathon, pushing my six-year-old daughter the entire distance in a jog stroller, while it rained three inches and sponges went floating down the street. It takes a real marathon romantic to appreciate the romance in this.

The man I married is Portland Marathon Race Director, Les Smith. I have watched his commitment to the Portland Marathon and the commitment of many other Portland Marathon Committee members. It seemed to me that a great and romantic history existed which few people knew about. This is the reason I have tried to capture the golden past of the Portland Marathon. The Portland Marathon is no different than the famous marathons we read about. The only thing that separates it from those famous marathons is that, until now, no one has written its history

A silvery end to a romanatic run: mylar space blankets keep finishers warm.

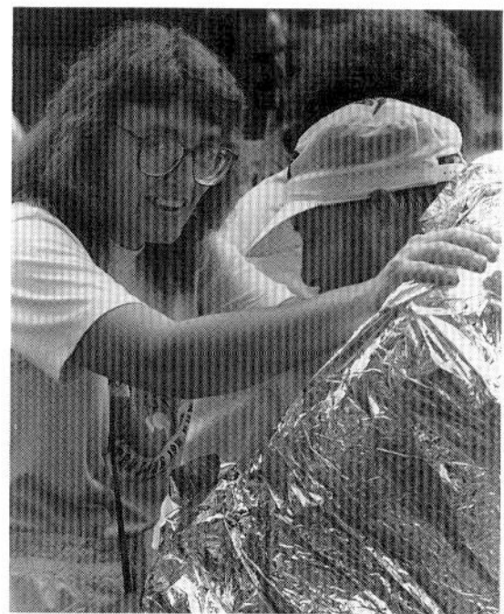

Director of the New York City Marathon. "It improves your sex life. Runners may or may not be better lovers, but I'll tell you this, more romances are launched on the running course than in singles bars."

310

THE STARTING LINE

From Athens, Greece, to Portland, Oregon

> *"If you want to run, then run a mile.*
> *If you want to experience another life,*
> *run a marathon."*
>
> Emil Zatopek
> Olympic Champion

The marathon we know today is inextricably tied to a solitary and grueling run that took place twenty-five hundred years ago in Greece. Pheidippides (fi-dip-e-deez) was the runner, and although Greek historians have recorded a number of conflicting accounts, the triumph of his achievement has illuminated the great race we call the marathon.

Supposedly, Pheidippides not only ran an enormously long distance in a very short time, he managed this over rugged terrain. Legend says that he fought with the Athenians at Marathon in a desperate and ultimately victorious battle against the Persians, then ran the twenty-five miles back to Athens to bring the news to the anxiously waiting city fathers, whereupon he "expired straight away" after gasping out his message.

According to the Greek historian, Herodotus, Pheidippides had already run to Sparta seeking help against the Persians. This is a little like running non-stop from Portland to Tillamook and back with major mountains in between. Herodotus, who says that Pheidippides accomplished this in less than forty-eight hours, naturally assumed that divine intervention had occurred. (Today, we might give credit to endomorphines.) Supposedly, the god Pan met Pheidippides on Mount Parthenium, where, much to the tired runner's dismay, the god badgered him with complaints about the Athenians. However, Pan also encouraged him to go the distance, and once the Athenians had recovered from the war, they built a shrine to Pan under the Acropolis and began holding annual ceremonies, with a torch race and animal sacrifices, to court Pan's protection and to honor the hero Pheidippides.

Two other ancient historians, Plutarch and Lucian, tell the same general story—a long run to bring news of the victory at Marathon—but disconcertingly, each historian credited a different runner. Plutarch named Eucles and pointed out that other historians had named Thersippus of Eroadae. Historian Lucian claimed that Philippides (possibly just a Greek typo) was the man who ran the distance, then collapsed

■Frenchmen Michael Breál and Baron Pierre de Coubertin originally proposed a long distance race for the first Olympic games. Inspired by the legend of Pheidippides, the Greeks immediately accepted the idea and quickly decided on its title - the *marathon*.

■**Author Jim Fixx speculated that**

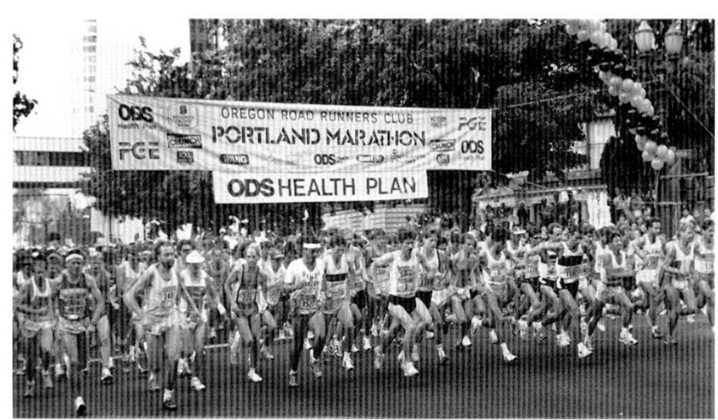

Olympic Marathon Distances and Results

Year	Location	Distance	Winner/Country	Time
1896	Athens	24 mi., 1500 yds.	Spyridon Louis/GRE	2:58:50
1900	Paris	25 miles	Michel Theato/FRA	2:59:45
1904	St. Louis	24 mi., 1500 yds.	Thomas Hicks/USA	3:28:63
1906	Athens	24 mi., 1500 yds.	William Sherring/CAN	2:51:23.6
1908	London	26 mi., 385 yds.	John Hayes/USA	2:55:18.4 OR
1912	Stockholm	24 mi., 1725 yds.	Kenneth McArthur/SAF	2:36:54.8
1916	NO OLYMPICS - WWI			
1920	Antwerp	26 mi., 990 yds.	Johannes Kolehmainen/FIN	2:32:35.8 WB
1924	Paris	26 mi., 385 yds.	Albin Stenroos/FIN	2:41:22.6
1928	Amsterdam	26 mi., 385 yds.	Bougheran El Ouafi/FRA	2:32:57.0
1932	Los Angeles	26 mi., 385 yds.	Juan Carlos Zabala/ARG	2:31:36.0 OR
1936	Berlin	26 mi., 385 yds.	Kee-Chung Sohn/JAP	2:29:19.2 OR
1940 and 1944 - NO OLYMPICS - WWII				
1948	London	26 mi., 385 yds.	Delfo Cabrero/ARG	2:34:51.6
1952	Helsinki	26 mi., 385 yds.	Emil Zatopek/CZE	2:23:03.2 OR
1956	Melbourne	26 mi., 385 yds.	Alain Minoun O'Kacho/FRA	2:25:00.0
1960	Rome	26 mi., 385 yds.	Bikila Abebe/ETH	2:15:16.2 WB
1964	Tokyo	26 mi., 385 yds.	Bikila Abebe/ETH	2:12:11.2 WB
1968	Mexico City	26 mi., 385 yds.	Mamo Wolde/ETH	2:20:26.4
1972	Munich	26 mi., 385 yds.	Frank Shorter/USA	2:12:19.8
1976	Montreal	26 mi., 385 yds.	Waldeman Cierpinski/GDR	2:09:55.0 OR
1980	Moscow	26 mi., 385 yds.	Waldeman Cierpinski/GDR	2:11:03.0
1984	M Los Angeles	26 mi., 385 yds.	Carlos Lopes/POR	2:09:21.0 OR
	F Los Angeles	26 mi., 385 yds.	Joan Benoit/USA	2:24:52 OR
1988	M Seoul	26 mi., 385 yds.	Gelindo Bordin/ITA	2:10:32 OR
	F Seoul	26 mi., 385 yds.	Rosa Mota/POR	2:25:39

*WB = World Best   OR = Olympic Record

Pheidippides died as a result of heat stroke, rather than a heart attack. This makes sense of the rumor that Pheidippides ran the distance in heavy armor. Ironically, Fixx also died while running — of congenital heart disease.

■The first Boston Marathon was held on April 19, 1897, a Monday, the day all subsequent Boston Marathons have been held. The first New York City Marathon took off on September 13, 1970.

■The 1924 Boston

dead. In sum, while no one is quite sure who ran, we are pretty sure that a run took place by someone between Athens and Marathon in 479 B.C.

All this may lead to the false impression that the ancient Greeks greatly favored long-distance running. In the ancient Olympic Games, no great distance races were included. The longest event was probably the "long course," which was a distance of about 2 3/4 miles. One of the winners of this run, Ladas, is remembered as the Greek who fell dead at the completion of his race. This is no great advertisement for Greek stamina or successful training methods, but their contributions to our modern marathon cannot be denied.

In 1896, when the Olympics were resurrected in Greece, a long-distance race of 24 3/4 miles was included in the program in tribute to Greek history. The race began at the city of Marathon and ended in Athens, and the name Marathon was given to the event. (Appropriately, the first Olympic winner was a Greek.)

In 1908, two miles were added to the run. This addition to a race that had already proved itself a grueling distance is difficult to explain. But during the reign of King Edward VII, Princess Alexandria heatedly insisted on viewing the finish of the marathon in front of the Royal Box. The marathon began at Windsor Castle. In order to have it start at the Castle and finish in front of the Royal Box at White City Stadium in London, its distance grew to 26.2 miles. That distance was established at the fifth running of the Olympic Marathon in 1908, and, to this date, no one has denied the King's Court its distance, and every marathon in the world has eventually adopted it.

Modern Marathoning

The marathon road from Athens to Portland was not a direct route. It went by way of many running tracks, over miles of long, lonely roads, and through the running communities of Boston, New York, and London. For years, the number of marathoners could be counted on several sets of toes. Then, in

Marathon was the first in the United States to conform to the 26-mile, 385-yard distance set by royal decree at the 1908 Olympic Games in London.

■Oregonian Alberto Salazar ran four consecutive marathons in under 2:10. No one else has run back-to-back marathons under 2:10. These were the first four marathons Salazar ever ran.

■When the exhausted Greek runner, Pheidippides, reached Athens to announce the battle's victory to the

Even children travel from abroad to participate in Portland's international event.

the 1970s, the United States experienced a running craze. Early mornings and late afternoons found runners adding to the scenery during rush-hour traffic. High school tracks were swamped with runners running round and round, looking at their stopwatches in hopes that the next lap would be better than the last. Social conversation at cocktail parties often centered on shoes, split times, and races.

Two of Oregon's most well-known cities, Eugene and Portland, enrolled much of their athletic populace in running clubs—all headed by the Oregon Road Runners Club (ORRC). In fact, during the 1970s and early 1980s, ORRC was one of the largest running clubs in the entire United States, sporting over 5,000 members.

A step behind the running revolution, marathoning began to come into vogue when Frank Shorter won the 1972 Olympic Gold Medal. Frank's victory, the first uncontested Olympic marathon win by the United States, gave impetus to the average runner. Shorter made the marathon look like a possibility. If Frank, a nice American boy, not the least bit godlike, could run a marathon, then it was not just for the physically elite. Mere mortals could also run a marathon, although not as fast as Frank's winning time of 2:12:19.8.

In the eighties, baby boomers became Yuppies, donned Nike running apparel, and drove Volvos to and from running tracks. Among these runners was the marathoner.

The marathoner endured not just 26 miles of physical calamity but also

Athenians, he cried "Nike!" Translated, this means "Hail! We are victorious!"

■Olympic Marathon gold medal winner Abebe Bikila had his appendix removed only five and a half weeks before the 1964 Olympic Marathon. Nevertheless, he won with a World Best time of 2:12:11.2 and

Sore knees won't stop the modern marathoner. ■ One runner hopes Batman gives him a flying start.

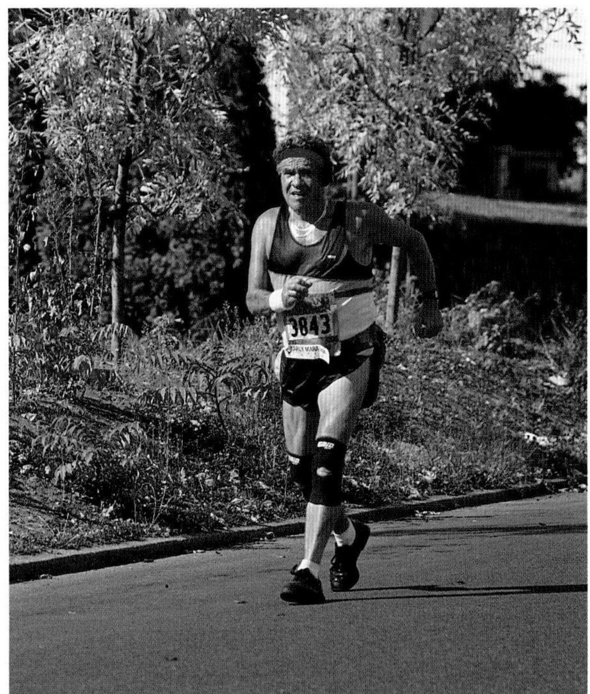

average only one to two years longer than his sedentary co-workers (albeit, healthier years). To the marathoner, it seemed (and still seems) that he could not just run, which is all he wanted to do, but that he had to justify his running, which he did not want to do.

Nevertheless, throughout the first sixty years of this century, the number of marathons slowly but steadily increased. Besides the Boston Marathon, many other prestigious marathons

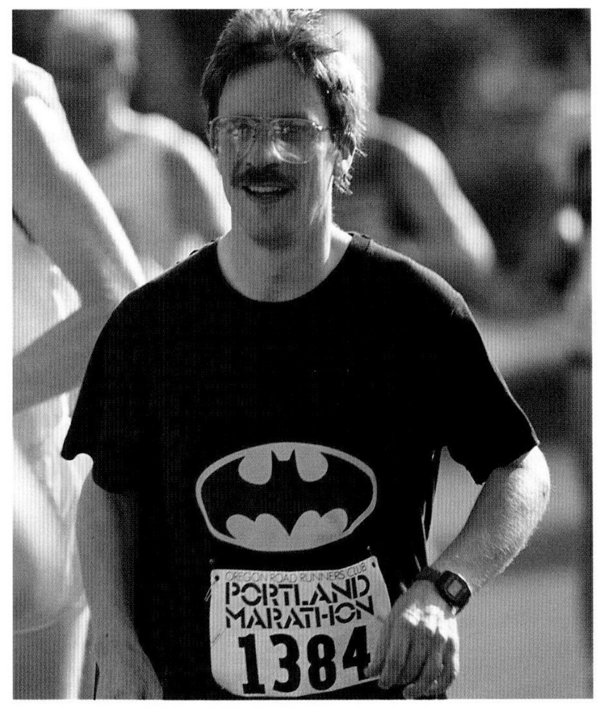

the ordeal of overcoming the non-marathoner's prejudices. The marathoner learned from prominent physicians that he was probably an obsessive personality (the running of marathons was cited as proof), that he was probably a Type-A personality, and that he was due for a not-too-distant heart attack if his running persisted. Simultaneously, he heard that he wouldn't have a heart attack but that despite his sweat he would live on an

became the first man to win the Olympic Marathon twice.

■**The second Olympic Games were held in Paris in 1900, and the French were as excited about having a local boy win as the Greeks had been four years earlier. But rumors immediately began to fly that winner Michel Theato had used his**

Trainers, coaches, even a gorilla take to the road to support the marathoner.

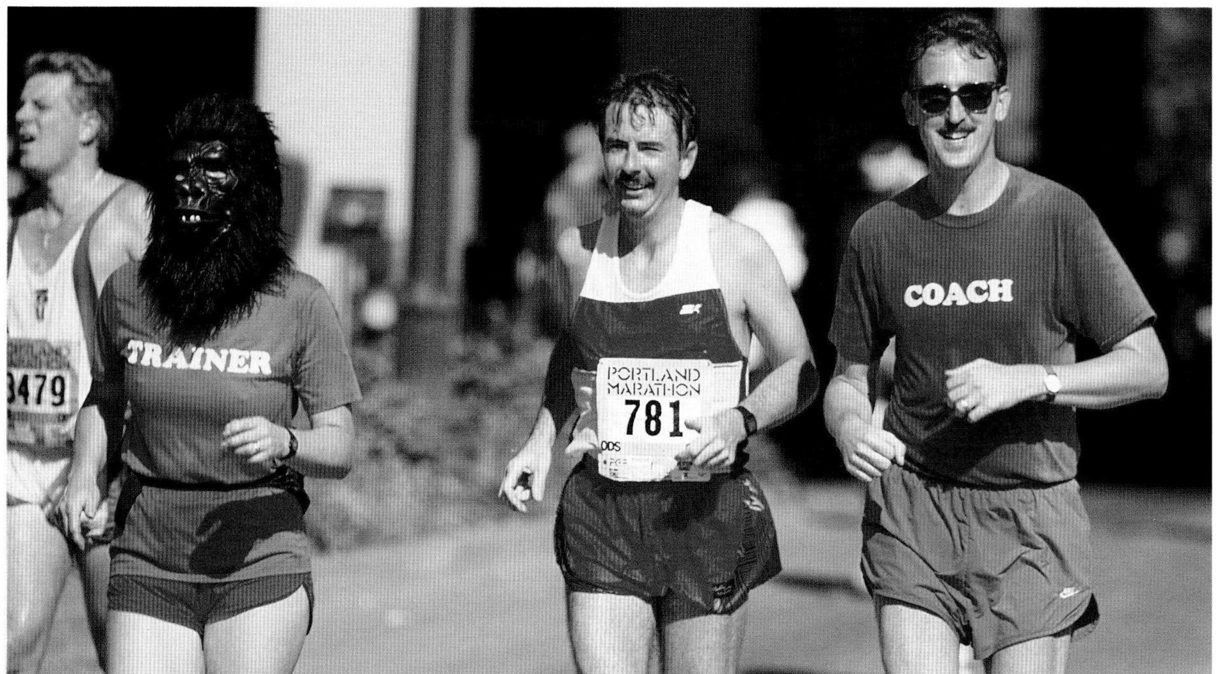

found their place within the annals of race history. The New York City Marathon was inaugurated in 1970; the Seaside Marathon in 1971; Grandma's Marathon in 1972; the Portland Marathon in 1972; Vancouver, B.C. in 1973; Honolulu in 1973; Nike-OTC Marathon in 1975; and there were many others.

Unfortunately, many people considered running a fad or just another opportunity to make money. In *The Running Revolution*, published in 1980, Joe Henderson battles these views. Henderson is a purist. As he so ardently points out, "Running has not changed much in the last 5,000 years." It is still one foot in front of the next and that is the way it should be. But as the eighties approached, Henderson saw that running had become much more than that. Runners had to justify running, and running had become big commercially. Runners were being pursued by people and groups who saw dollar signs. Much

considerable knowledge of local topography to complete the 25-mile Marathon by taking short cuts. His win was challenged but not

changed.

■The Rome Olympics in 1960 provided a number of firsts. It was the first Olympic Marathon that neither started nor finished

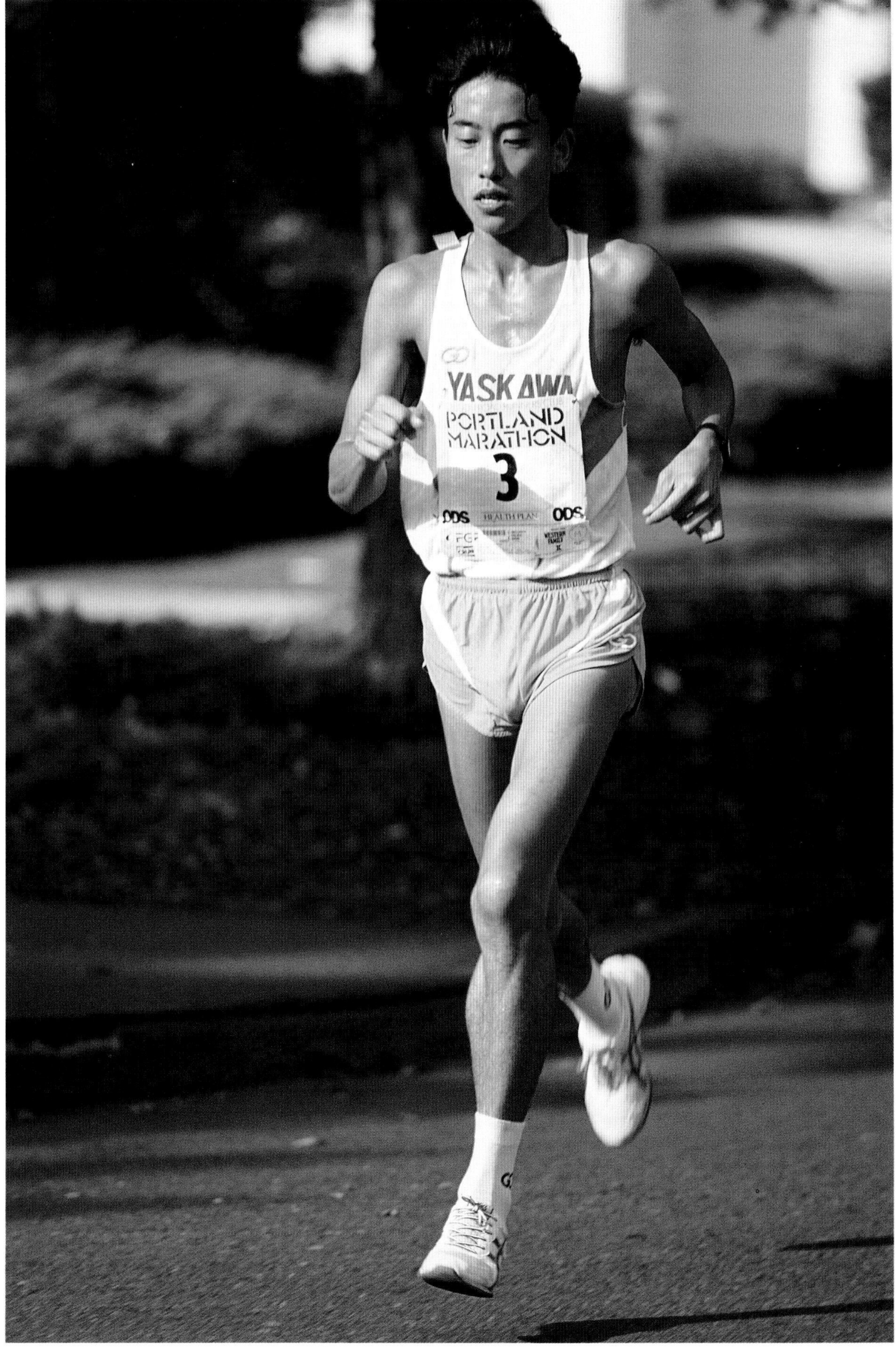
YASKAWA
PORTLAND
MARATHON
3
ODS
HEALTH PLAN
ODS

of this was due to "the running craze of the seventies." Joe observes that 5,000 runners participated in the Bay to Breakers in San Francisco in 1976, while in 1984 there were an estimated 30,000 people who ran, and there have been as many as 100,000 since then.

Henderson concluded, "We'd rather see 100,000 people running a mile in eight minutes, and no one watching, than have 100,000 watch one man break 3:50." In Portland and in other parts of the country, runners have headed toward a version of Joe Henderson's vision. They have become marathoners and they have combined intensely individual personal desires with a certain amount of necessary marathon commercialization.

A curious man once asked a mountain climber, "Why do you climb the mountain?" The famous response, "Because it's there," reflects the marathoner's feelings as well. Today we have mountain climbers looking for the best mountain, and marathoners looking for the best marathon. The challenge to race officials is to produce the best marathon they can so that Sunday morning runners and professionals will have an event to attend that helps them achieve their personal goal.

Marathoners like to discuss marathons. At the New York City Marathon in 1989, two of them analyzed marathoners of the late 1980s. Being long on running and short on words, they came to some quick but accurate conclusions. They observed that today's marathoners were very serious about completing the distance they had set for themselves. They pointed out that they would participate only in prestigious marathon events that provided them with the best possible situation and that marathons that could not furnish this had either disbanded due to lack of support or were declining in number of participants. Finally, they noted that the most rigorous of American marathons, the Boston Marathon, had shown its support of the average runner by lowering its qualifying times.

Man first learns to crawl, then to walk, and then to run. But the marathon does not only mean to run.

within a stadium; the first to finish by moonlight; and the first in which the winner ran barefoot.

■In 1972, the AAU gave women the go-ahead to run marathons, but told them they had to start the race ten minutes ahead of the men. At the 1972 New York Marathon, Nina

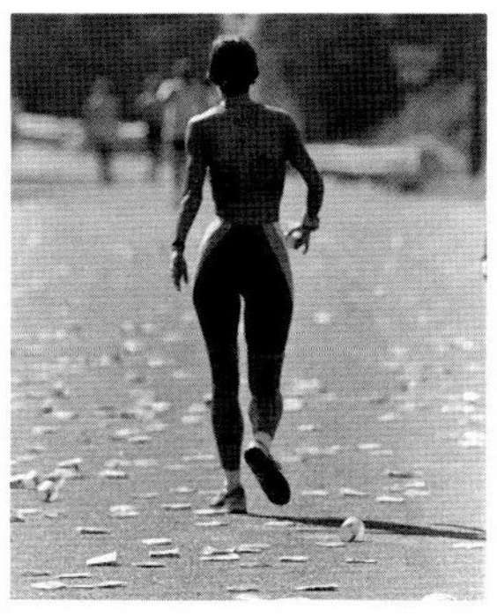

Kuscsik refused and led a sit-in, and the female athletes started with the men. Officials added ten minutes to the women's finish times, but the rule was

When marathoning started as an event in the 1896 Olympics, marathoning was likened to running a long distance very fast. Today we have a long distance—26.2 miles—but running it very fast is not necessarily the definition of marathoning. Today, *going the distance* is the active description. We have people completing the distance at a walk, a jog, in a wheelchair, and on crutches. At the 1988 Portland Marathon, the city witnessed the closest thing to a person crawling a marathon as will probably ever be seen. A woman amputee completed the distance attached to a skateboard. Her time was not fast, but she showed the spirit of every marathoner who chooses to go the distance.

Women, You Too Can Do 26.2

As soon as men started running marathons, they began believing only they could. That is, those of the male gender believed they were capable of running great distances and the weaker, gentler female was not.

During the first seventy-five years of the twentieth century, books, pamphlets, and articles warned that running was dangerous for women. It was believed that they could do permanent

never applied again.

■Roberta (Bobbi) Gibb ran the Boston Marathon before Katherine Switzer but was not harassed as Switzer was a couple of

years later, probably because officials did not notice her. Bobbi also ran the Boston Marathon the same year as Switzer, but race referees only challenged

damage to their "internals" if they partook in this extremely demanding exercise, if they ran, that is, any distance greater than a 220, which is half a lap around a 1/4-mile track. This was the longest distance women ran in the Olympics prior to 1968. (They competed just once in a 5,000 meter race in the 1928 Olympics.)

Patti Finke, an exercise physiologist who organizes, with husband Warren, the Portland Marathon Training Clinics, smiles as she recalls some of the beliefs of bygone days. Laughs Patti, "They thought that a woman's uterus would fall out if she ran too fast, too far, or too much." Patti is a perfect example of how wrong they were. She has run over forty marathons, completed approximately twenty ultramarathons, and has both her uterus and a full grown son.

Based on limited medical knowledge and general prejudices, the Amateur Athletic Union (AAU), which in 1978 became The Athletics Congress (TAC), had a policy that prohibited women from competing in distance races. This ruling included marathons and meant that a women's Olympic Marathon was out of the question, even though some marathon race directors began allowing women to run in their races as early as the mid-sixties.

An argument in favor of the AAU stance cited the 1928 Olympics, when, during the 5,000 Meter track event, one of the women competitors fainted and collapsed. Marathon officials and members of the AAU interpreted this as evidence that women lacked stamina and could not run long distances, but from what we now know, it seems likely that this particular woman may not have been allowed to run enough distances to properly prepare for the race. And, when we look back at marathon history at the death of Pheidippides, forbidding women to run a distance race because they might collapse doesn't quite make sense. However, following this event, Olympic officials abolished lengthy races for women. It would be years before officials changed their stand.

America's oldest marathon, the Boston Marathon, is sprinkled with

Katherine.

■**In 1975, Jacqueline Hansen became the first woman to win a marathon in less than two hours and forty minutes. Five years**

later, seven different women broke the imposing 2:30 mark.

■Judy Ikenberry, who courageously fought AAU discrimination against women, won the

stories of women who tried to run the event and who were thrown off the course and admonished by officials. There are tales of women who entered the marathon through the proper registration process and were pulled from the starting line once their sex was revealed. One of the most memorable registered herself as K. Switzer. When officials realized that K. was not a man, they pulled her number, jerked her off the course, and gave her a stiff reprimand. To her credit, that did not prevent her from running on the sidewalks as a "bandit" and clocking her own time for the distance. Switzer served as a role model for many women marathon runners.

Throughout the sixties, more and more women ran marathons as bandits. The term bandit has applied to two types of runners over the course of the years. One meaning, still current, describes a runner who has not paid his entry fee. The second described a woman running in an event in which, due to her sex, she was not supposed to compete. The biggest difference between the two types is that female bandits would have welcomed the opportunity to pay the registration fee and receive an official running number. But it was not until the late sixties and early seventies that marathon organizers began allowing women to enter their races, and this was only due to some heroic efforts by both men and women.

Judy Ikenberry (who along with husband Dennis runs the computerized finish-line race results at the Portland Marathon) is an example of a woman who ran for the sheer pleasure of running and with her husband's help paved the road for female runners. Judy's running career took off in the sixties, when she was invited to participate in the Women's Olympic Qualifying Trials in Abilene, Texas, for the Half Mile Event at the Olympic Games, which would be held later that year in Rome. Judy came in fifth at the trials and for the next ten years she competed in track events and road races. Slowly, as maturing runners do, she developed a fancy for longer distances, for long road races, and, finally, for the marathon.

first national AAU Women's Marathon championship in 1974 by running a 2:55:40.

■**At the 1984 Olympic Games in Los Angeles, the first Olympics to**

offer a marathon event to women, Joan Benoit of the United States crossed the finish line in a time of 2:24:52 to take the gold.

■Twenty-five percent of

Always a colorful run, the Portland Marathon has one of the highest percentages of women in the nation.

Portland's Marathon entrants are female runners. This makes them one of the largest contingents of women runners in the entire nation.

■Women usually comprise 50% of the Portland Marathon 5-Miler. This is one of the highest percentages of female runners in a five mile event anywhere in the nation.

■Julie Neupert did not start running marathons until her daughter was two. She says, "Next to childbirth, marathoning is the most physically

First and second place 1989 women's winners, Debra Meyer (75) and Heather Tolford (77), joyfully surge ahead.

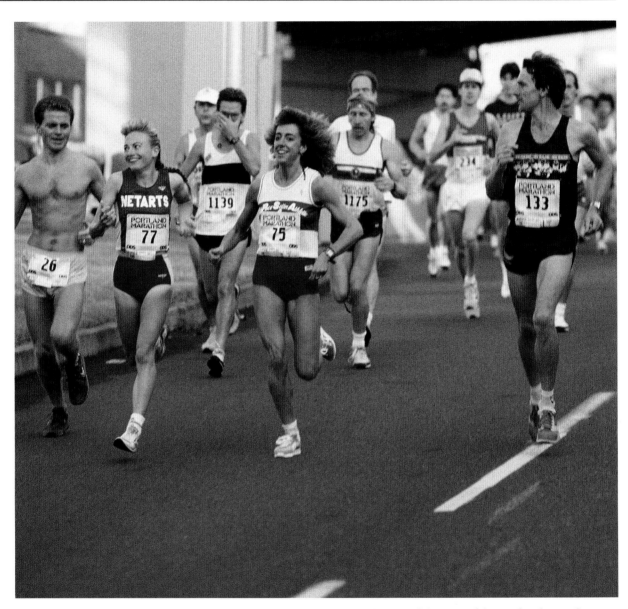

Reflecting on some of her running antics throughout this period, Judy says that she and her girlfriends thought it was fun to run a marathon without

demanding and emotionally rewarding thing I've ever done."

■For all the hype surrounding women's entry into the marathon, it is unfortunate that it was a woman who was first caught cheating at two major marathons. In November, 1979, Rosie Ruiz hopped the subway for part of her

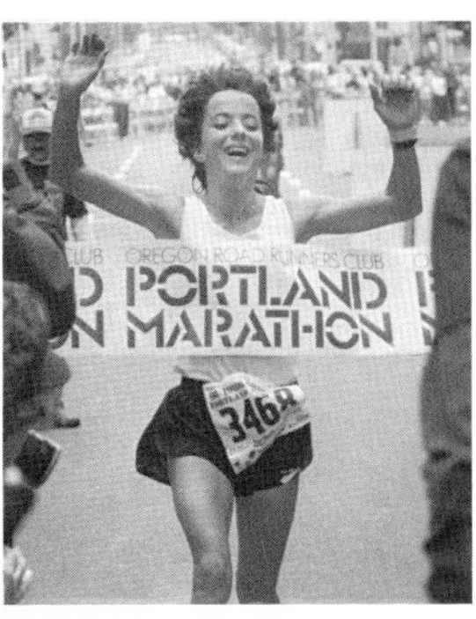

getting thrown off the course. They were running for the joy of running.

In 1970, Judy and her friend, Lyn Carmen, were asked to compete in the Las Vegas Marathon. Offered twenty dollars per day spending money plus hotel accommodations, they thought they had made the big time. Both women realized this was an unprecedented offer to female runners. They did not realize the potential seriousness of their adventure until Dennis received a phone call from the local AAU chairman in Southern California who warned, "If Judy and Lyn run the Las Vegas Marathon, you will be barred from all AAU-sanctioned events for life."

"Start the legal machinery," replied Judy's proud and defiant husband. "They're running." Dennis, Judy, and Lyn were all members of the Pasadena Athletic Association, as well as Olympic hopefuls, and the contamination clause within the AAU rules book could ruin not only them but the entire Pasadena Association. The Ikenberrys, with the PAA's whole-hearted support, braced themselves for a legal battle.

Judy and Lyn ran Las Vegas, but, oddly enough, nothing ever came of it. The AAU must have reviewed the running scene throughout the nation and come to the conclusion that if women wanted to run marathons, and men were behind them, they should. By 1970, hundreds of women had safely completed marathons. The AAU formally changed its stand on the issue in 1972, and the Olympics finally offered a Women's Marathon at the 1984 Games in Los Angeles.

Interestingly, the Portland Marathon never did draw a distinction between male and female runners. From its beginnings in 1972, all the Marathon ever wanted was runners. Almost twenty years later, Portland can boast an event that is among the top five in the nation in its number of female participants. Women make up almost one quarter of its field.

Today, women's world record finish times for the marathon are short of men's finish times by only 14 minutes, and both men and women have the green light for marathoning.

marathon distance in New York. This qualified her for the most prestigious race in the country, Boston. In 1980, in Boston, she jumped into the race

half a mile from the finish. Crowned with the winner's laurel wreath, she had people convinced for some time that she had really won it.

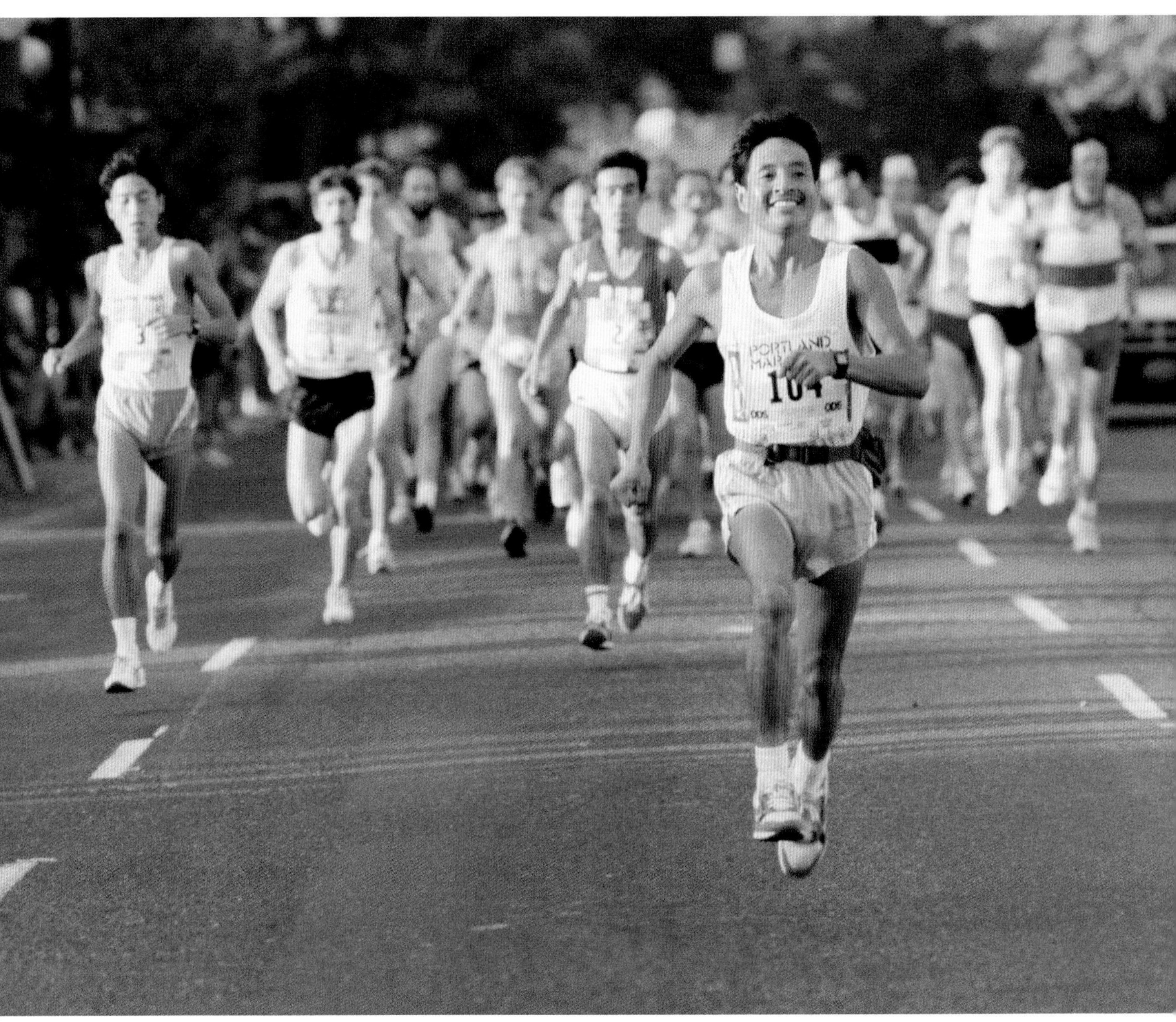
PORTLAND
104

SETTING THE PACE

The Portland Marathon Takes Off

> *"This race may serve as the country's best model for the potential of an all-volunteer, all-amateur marathon."*
>
> *Joe Henderson*
> *Running author and commentator*

The Portland Marathon Race Director put himself to bed the night prior to the big day, satisfied that all that could be done in preparation had been done. He knew sleep would come more easily for him than for the runners anticipating the race, and his sleep was sound. The late November weather offered a quiet night. There were no pounding raindrops on the roof, no howling winds to interrupt a night of needed rest. Early next morning, his dreams were broken by the ringing of the phone.

"Are you the race director," a masculine voice asked.

"Yes, I am."

"Have you looked outside?"

Bill Gorman rubbed the sleep from his eyes, lifted the curtains on the window next to his bed, blinked, and looked again in disbelief. What he saw was not typical Thanksgiving weather. There were two inches of snow on the ground.

"Are you still having the Marathon today?"

"Absolutely," Bill replied.

Like a good drama, the show must go on. Sixty-six years after the advent of the first Olympic Marathon and several thousand years after Pheidippides ran the distance, the Oregon Road Runners Club (ORRC) followed suit. Under the leadership of Ken Weidkamp, the Portland Marathon took to the road in 1972, raising the curtain on what was to become one of the most highly rated marathons in the nation.

In its comparatively brief history, the Portland Marathon experienced dramatic struggles and a colorful set of triumphs and tragedies. A review of the past reveals a large group of dedicated ORRC and Marathon Committee members, all heroically led by an unpaid race director, nursing the Marathon through its times of turmoil and cheering it through its moments of glory.

From the onset, the biggest struggle confronting the Portland Marathon was location. In other words, over what 26.2 miles of city streets would hundreds of marathoners stream? Visionaries from the running community could see the potential success of a marathon held downtown. City officials and police could see only catastrophe. The city

■The start of the 1989 Portland Marathon was temporarily short-circuited by a tree branch, which fell across two power terminals, blowing the fuses in main and back-up amplifiers at the start line. Electricity was not restored, and a hand-held bull horn had to be substituted.

■The political climate of the Philippines rarely affects the Portland Marathon, but in 1983 the finisher medals minted there did not arrive until well after the race due

Sauvie Island Course

year	race director	finishers
1972	Ken Weidkamp	173*
1973	Ken Weidkamp	161
1974	Bill Gorman	213
1975	Bill Gorman	246
1976	Bill Gorman	406

*50% were half-marathoners

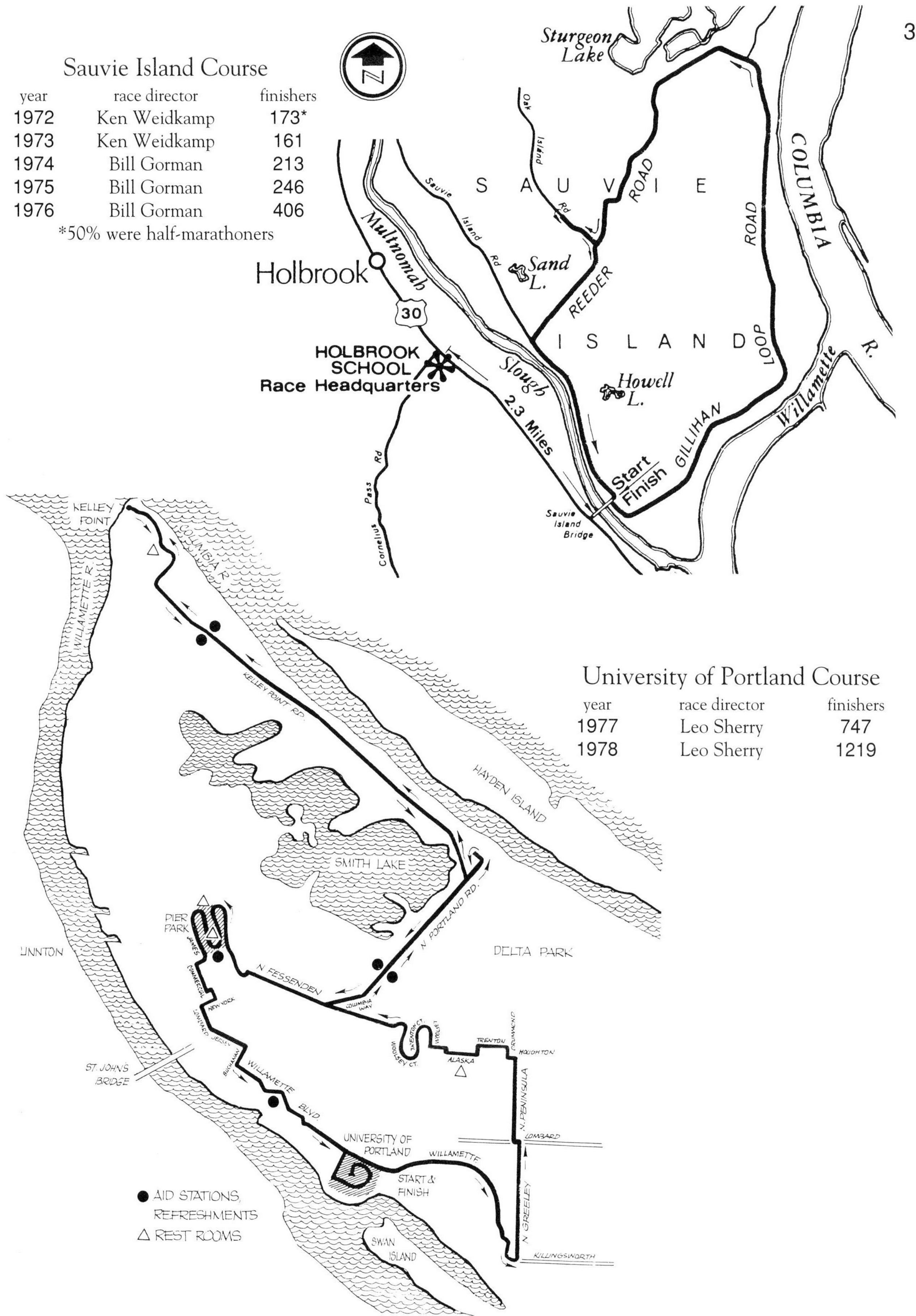

University of Portland Course

year	race director	finishers
1977	Leo Sherry	747
1978	Leo Sherry	1219

prevailed, and Ken Weidkamp, who had designated himself race director early in 1972 with the blessings of ORRC, set out to find a course outside the city that was agreeable to bureaucrats and runners. For runners, this meant a course with both alluring scenic beauty and fast finish times. The result: the first Marathon was held on an island. Held on Sauvie Island, in fact, just seven miles west of Portland.

The Island Marathon promised runners good times with its fairly flat, double 12-mile loop and small 2.2 mile dog-leg. With old farm houses, pastures of farm animals, and croplands, surrounded entirely by fresh water, and located where the Willamette River meets the Columbia River, the island reflected its pastoral history. Tales of Indian tribes and early settlers pepper its memoirs. To runners, officials, and race committee members, Sauvie Island seemed to be the ideal location.

The Multnomah County Sheriff's Department agreed there would not be many traffic obstacles. Ken Weidkamp, knowing that the independent islanders would want to give the Marathon their blessing, attended Sauvie Island Grange Hall meetings and, with the support of a strong member of the community, Mr. George Douglas, obtained most of the islanders' cooperation. Unfortunately, a minority of islanders, unenthusiastic about runners swamping their roads, expressed their dissatisfaction in a variety of ways. The most memorable incident required a Multnomah County Sheriff's officer to ticket a local islander trying to run Marathon participants off the road with his pick-up.

Episodes like this prompted the Marathon committee to find a new course. As well, numbers had increased so much that the logistics of parking became impossible. Both Weidkamp and Gorman had hired Evergreen Stages to run shuttles from Holbrook School, which is located near the junction of U.S. 30 and Cornelius Pass Road, to the start on Sauvie Island to avoid parking problems, but as the Marathon grew, even shuttles could not handle the load.

Weidkamp, who served the Marathon during 1972 and 1973, and

to political unrest that later ousted Ferdinand Marcos.

■Almost 1.7 million dollars is spent downtown during Marathon Week.

Approximately 25,000 spectators show up on race day to watch the events.

■In 1972, the first Portland Marathon was not won by local

Reflections of past marathoners dapple the University of Portland course.

Portlanders, despite a possible home-court advantage. Winners Jim Pearson and Susan Rossiter hailed from Bellingham, Washington. They

earned respective finish times of 2:25:41 and 3:27:53.

■Almost 70% of the Portland Marathon's runners live out of town, arriving by

Gorman, race director from 1974 to 1976, were both active in finding another course. After a tremendous amount of work and research by Leo Sherry, who became race director in 1977, course certifier and logistics man, Ralph Davis, and an unsung hero, Tom James from the city's Traffic Engineering department, the ever-expanding Marathon left the island and in 1977 edged into Portland.

The Marathon had experienced considerable participant growth in its first five years. Opening with almost two hundred runners, the Marathon saw almost 800 runners make their way to its new course at the University of Portland. This figure was double the previous year's record on the island, when 425 runners registered and 406 finished, establishing the Marathon as one of the top five in the United States based on number of participants.

The challenge of numbers was one the University of Portland could easily solve. There would be no need for tedious and sometimes desperate transportation measures, and restroom facilities were plentiful. The University of Portland course saw another growth spurt when 1219 runners finished the course its second year.

But these numbers apparently dismayed the University of Portland. Unhappy with the wear and tear its facilities received on race day, the university bowed out as host, forcing Leo Sherry to scramble to another course during his third year as race director. Working once again with city traffic engineer, Tom James, and dedicated ORRC members, Sherry mapped out a route which started and finished at the Multnomah County Expo Center in Delta Park. The city approved, but runners were unhappy. Five hundred fewer runners finished that year, and the uncertainty created by another course change and continued bad weather were blamed.

Sherry had probably not imagined the unpaid position of race director could be so tough. He had agreed to take the job while swept up in race euphoria. During the Marathon's last year on the island, Leo ran the

plane, train, and automobile from states around the country. Fourteen nations were represented in 1989.

■**Many people don't understand why an entry fee higher than $5.00 is necessary. To clarify: it costs the Portland Marathon approximately $36 per runner to hold the**

Lead runners stream away from the start line on the 1980 Delta Park course.

Marathon with his 16-year-old daughter, Ann. Ann Sherry had never run a marathon and she was the youngest female entrant. Her dad knew she was a talented athlete but he never expected her to win. But win she did. With a time of 3:04:09, Ann Sherry was the first woman across the finish line. And, when Bill Gorman asked Leo to be race director the following year, he enthusiastically agreed.

Brent James, who followed in Sherry's footsteps as race director number four, claims he was tricked by ORRC board member and club treasurer, Les Smith, to be the acting race director for the 1980 event. He was a fanatic runner and he grappled with the problems as they arose.

Using the same course at the Multnomah County Expo Center in Delta Park, Brent moved up the date of the event by one more week, hoping that a late October race would solve weather problems. In spite of this safeguard, the course is most often remembered for its foul conditions. Stories of cold, wet, and chilled marathoners, aborting their runs in the face of rain and gale force winds, are legion. Natural adversity was abetted by human error when the lead police motorcyclist misdirected the pack of front runners, adding one and a half miles to the course for the first nineteen unlucky marathoners. (Lionel Ortega ran a 28-mile record time of 2:28:21.) Ironically, because it was confined and relatively free of traffic problems, city engineers and police

race.

■Patti Finke ran the 1978 Portland Marathon in a freezing, thick fog and was unable to find the course once she entered Pier Park. Although she was wearing a bright red turtleneck and Danskin tights, she knew no one could see her because she could not see anyone else. Only the

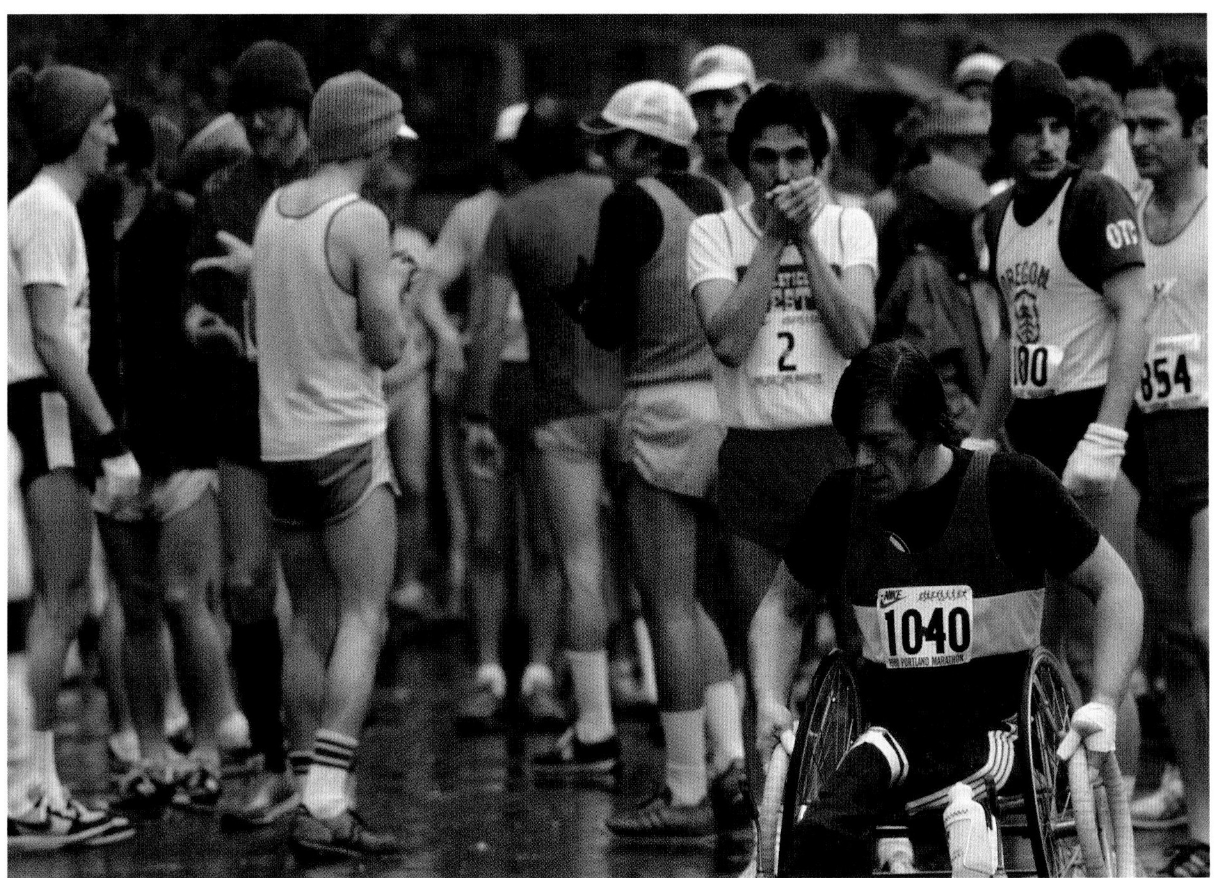

Portland's September date almost assures sunshine. Years past, a wet Marathon didn't faze the really dedicated.

officials all thought this Marathon was highly successful.

The history of the Portland Marathon could be regarded as a long-term campaign to bring the Marathon downtown. The Expo Center was used only twice, and the untiring efforts of Sherry, James, and their cohorts brought the course closer to the center of town. However, just as the logistics of city traffic was slowly being solved, race officials faced another problem: regaining the confidence of the runners.

Since its inception, the Portland Marathon had tried to follow the nation's running trends. But more and

sound of running feet and heavy breathing guided her.

■**When the city redesigned Front Avenue in 1986, it prevented the**

Marathon from reaching an artery vital to the race. Undaunted, the Marathon managed to have a thousand foot-long avenue built without taxpayer money. Naturally, it is called Marathon Avenue and is used exclusively for the event.

■The Portland

more marathons had become available throughout the Northwest, including the very popular Seaside Marathon, the Nike-OTC (Oregon Track Club), and several Seattle-area marathons. Runners naturally chose marathons that gave them the best running experience. While the Portland Marathon was struggling with course and date changes, which made nonsense of its race history and made comparisons in running times impossible, runners discovered they had other options.

Meanwhile, the city continued to drag its heels. It waited so long to approve the first course to enter the downtown area that it delayed crucial event advertising. The expression "they lost the battle but won the war" seems apropos. The Portland Marathon would finally win its war with the city, but its battle for marathoners was lost. A race that could not settle on a yearly date or location made runners uneasy, and the race experienced a five-year-low of 481 in 1981.

At the same time, it was becoming more and more difficult for the Marathon to support itself solely through entry fees. A constant bone of contention between race directors and ORRC board members, the Marathon's original entry fee was $4.00. In the Marathon's first eight years that fee increased by just one dollar. When committee members wanted to provide more for the runners during race day, including basic necessities such as food at the finish, etc., they had to find outside means, so race directors began looking for sponsors. G.I. Joe's helped out in Sherry's era, as did Adidas. Encouraged by Brent James, Nike helped out for five years, providing printed T-shirts, race numbers, and safety pins. They also stuffed the goody bags with Nike discount coupons.

But sponsors are not to be confused with donors. The Marathon from its beginning had donors to help with water and cups on the course, but it had no major help with the really big bills. In the Marathon's earlier years, companies such as Western Family and Thriftee Thriftway gave some of the food at the finish area. In 1982, U.S. Bank became the first cash sponsor.

Marathon may be the only marathon in the country that sends Christmas cards to all of its runners and volunteers. Masters World Record holder and artist Clive Davies always designs the cards.

■**The starting banner often inspires hysterical last-minute searches. Committee**

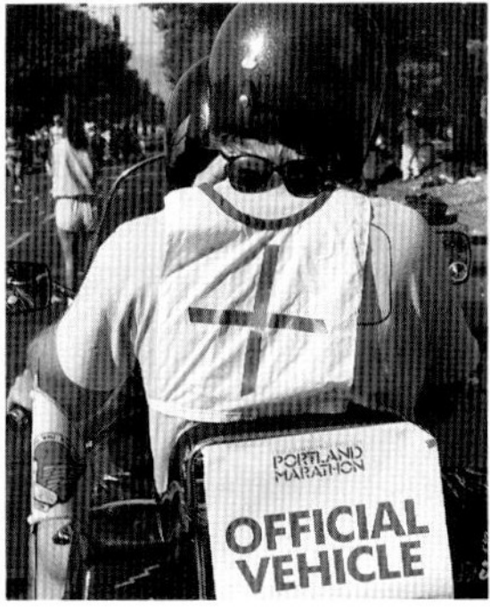

But on the whole, the Marathon remained largely self-supportive.

ORRC board member Kurt Hartung, who officially took over the Marathon in 1981, found his time as race director plagued by the same problems: he had to change the location of the course and regain the confidence of runners. Naturally, he also faced the old problem of obtaining city course approval.

Weather was still an ongoing problem. Originally, the Sauvie Island Marathon had taken place over the long Thanksgiving holiday. Alas, unpredictable weather conditions made it very unreliable, and marathoners had run a gauntlet of snow flurries, gale force winds, and torrential downpours, with only a little chilly, beautiful weather thrown in. Since then, the Marathon had moved steadily back in the autumn calendar. Now, Hartung had a group of people on his race committee, himself included, review weather patterns in Portland for the past twenty years. "Not that that has any significance on Portland weather," reflected Hartung.

They decided that early October seemed to provide consistently good weather. In 1981, an early October Marathon was run, and then, in 1984, under ORRC President Les Smith's influence, the race was stepped back one more week to the last weekend in September to take advantage of Portland's very best weather.

Kurt Hartung continued to work closely with traffic engineer Tom James. After much effort, a new course was created for the 1981 Marathon. Pushing closer to downtown, it started at the Memorial Coliseum and traveled through the Northwest section of Portland before finishing on Flint Street across from the coliseum. This course was rather circuitous. It had over 130 turns and shared some streets with railroad tracks. Unfortunately, attendance had bottomed out.

It was now that a man who had long figured in the Northwest running scene jumped into Marathon organizing with both feet. That man was Les Smith.

An ardent runner, Les Smith began running marathons in 1976. By 1981, he had started and completed fifteen.

members Jim Schaeffer and Susan Leonti suggest a treasure hunt may be the answer: runners could hunt for the thirty-foot-long banner before starting the race.

■The first Sauvie Island Marathon was so wet, runners were accused of having webbed feet.

■It is an established fact that most

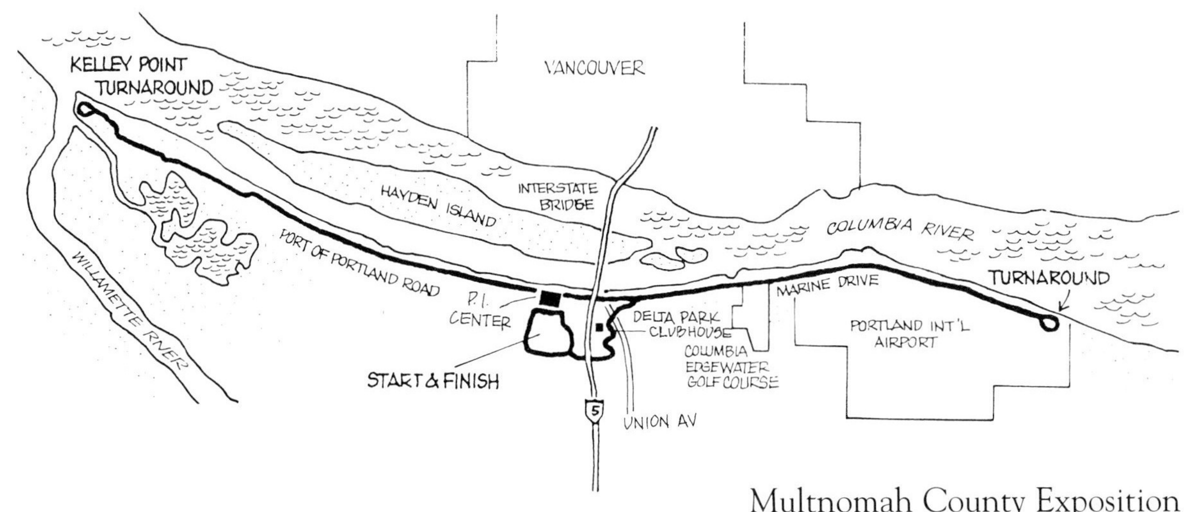

Multnomah County Exposition Center Course

year	race director	finishers
1979	Leo Sherry	792
1980	Brent James	841

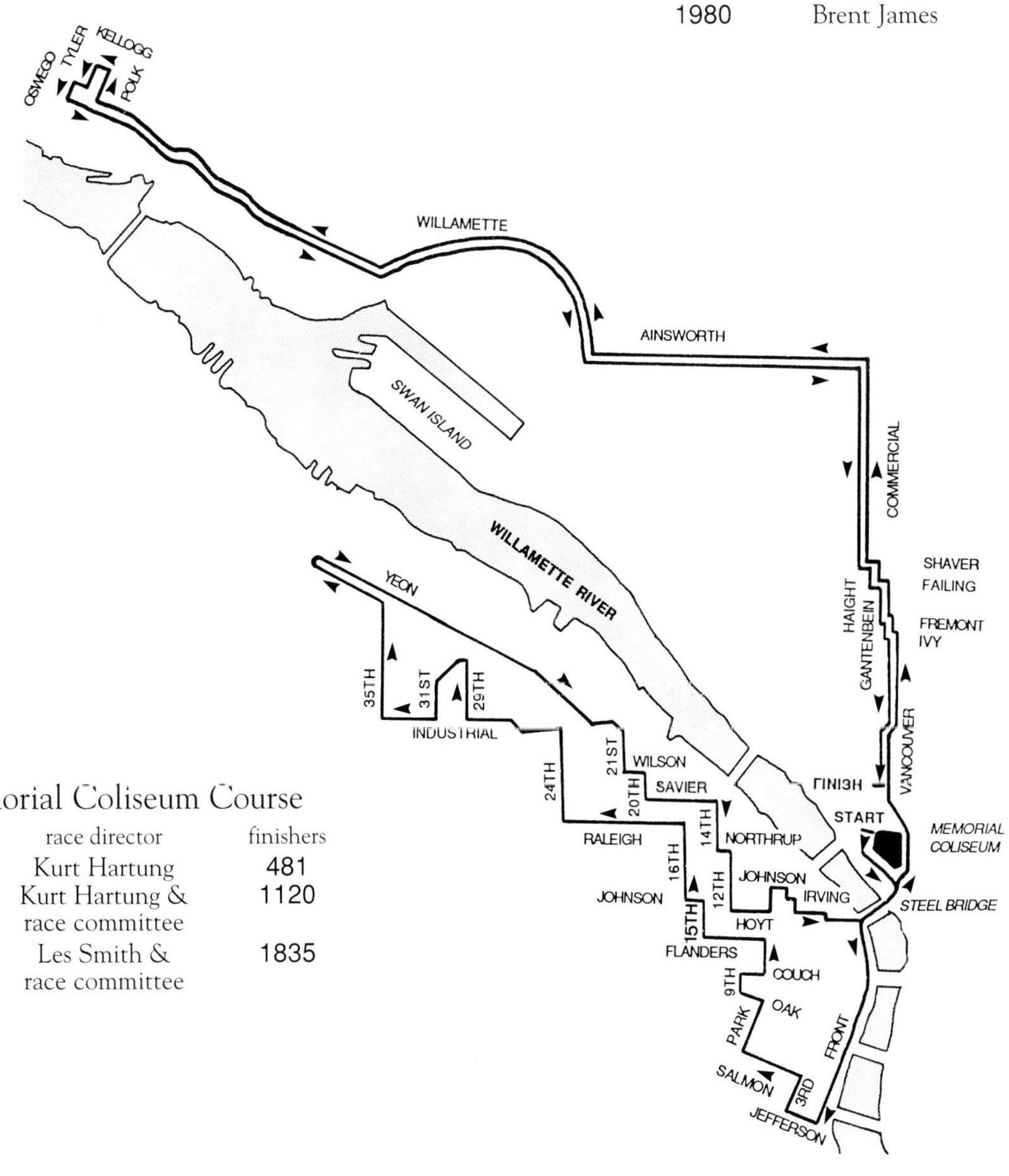

Memorial Coliseum Course

year	race director	finishers
1981	Kurt Hartung	481
1982	Kurt Hartung & race committee	1120
1983	Les Smith & race committee	1835

A healthy, active runner, he bragged about all the things runners brag about—low cholesterol, low body fat, low heart rate. He was completing his marathons in around 3:45.

But in 1981, while running the Portland Marathon, Les Smith decided to quit. At mile thirteen, halfway through a good run on a cool, clear October day, Les quit running. He quit because he had high expectations and a deep sense of responsibility.

At the time, Les was president of Oregon Road Runners Club, and the Portland Marathon was an ORRC event. Smith believed that all the events ORRC organized should be first class and as he ran that Marathon in 1982 he realized that ORRC could be doing much more for the runners. He imagined the Portland Marathon as an event above and beyond the world-renowned marathons he had participated in to date. He was experiencing a runner's high, but his ideas were solid.

Hoping to make the Marathon a little more tolerable for the runners behind him, Les quit running to help out at an undermanned aid station. He spent the remainder of the race pouring water and yelling words of encouragement to the rest of the field of runners as they passed by.

Long after the Marathon was over, and his runner's high had left him, Smith continued to imagine a marathon known worldwide for giving all runners the VIP treatment that only the front runners usually receive. He wanted a marathon where "Everyone is a winner." With this motto, he became the Race Director of the Portland Marathon in 1984. A labor relations attorney when not working on the Marathon, he proved himself to be a man of high expectations and achievements.

Les Smith's active involvement with the Marathon began in 1982 in his capacity as President of ORRC. (He did not actually take the position of race director until two years later, when he left office as ORRC president.) When Kurt Hartung stepped down as director, Les decided to completely reorganize the event by obtaining sponsors, increasing participation, and further

marathoners are between the ages of thirty and forty. This is one sport where people seem to do better—when they're older. This is because older athletes do better running an LSD (long, slow distance). Younger athletes excel at sprints. In an odd quirk, over half the field in the first

Among many tapped for duty, a Portland policeman points the way.

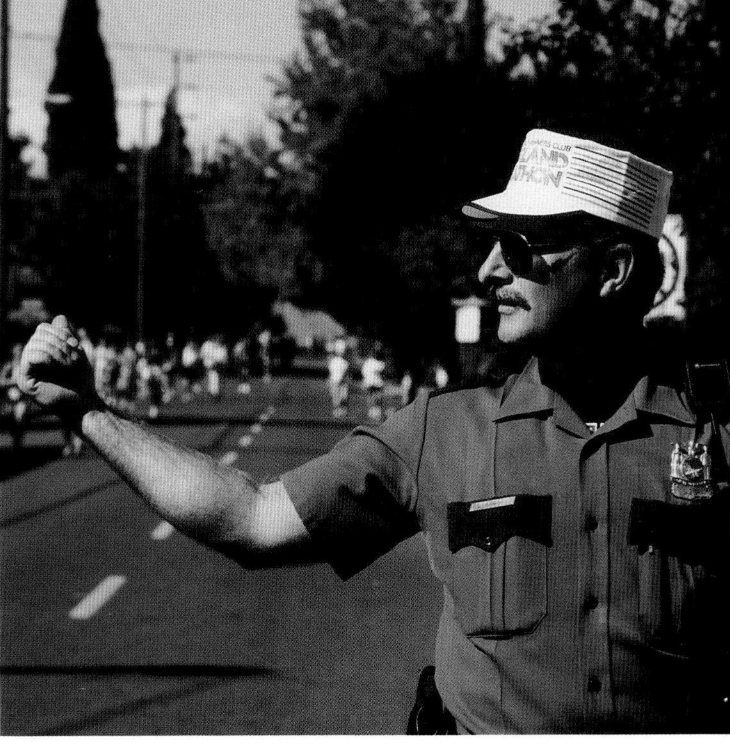

refining the course. Aware he could not accomplish all of these goals in one year, he decided to rebuild the race as an event with a broad base piece by piece. Using the best ideas from other marathons and road races around the world, he slowly saw his goals realized.

His new committee was a tight-knit group of dedicated people, some of them ORRC board members. These were people with professional know-how (attorneys and accountants); technical expertise (engineers and runners); fund-raising experience; and political clout. He continued to add highly qualified persons to the Marathon committee, all unpaid, as was he.

In 1982, the number of entrants doubled over the previous year. The race was run the last Sunday in September, and the weather was perfect. In 1983, the same Memorial Coliseum course was used, and there were no weather or traffic problems. After years of working with city engineers and police, the Marathon finally proved the race could be safely run.

Finally, in 1984, thanks to the hard work of many people, including course logistics manager John Gardner, the Portland Marathon arrived at its present location in the heart of downtown. This course has only twenty-seven turns and boasts a fast negative split.

Like his predecessors, Les Smith is an innovative race director. He has concentrated on generating sponsors and on providing as many services to runners as possible. Working with the

Portland Marathon was under nineteen.

■Since the Portland Marathon moved to its current course with its fast negative split, runners have believed that a marathon world record could be set if world class marathoners were to run here.

■Sister marathons are being born around the world. The Beppu-Oita

Manaichi Marathon in Japan was the first to become Portland's sister marathon. Marathons in Russia, East Germany, London, and Paris are all

Portland Marathon Committee

Les Smith ■ Race Director
Mamie Amundson, RN, ■ Medical Coordinator
Tanya Archer ■ Walk
Dennis Bromka ■ Finish Food/Entertainment
Dick Busby ■ Course Coordinator
Tony Capone ■ Photographer
Tim Cary ■ Logistics
Bruce Cheney ■ Communications
Vince Chiotti ■ Course Monitors/Westside
Luci Chiotti ■ Design
Mary Clifford ■ Kids' Run
Debbie Cook ■ Registrar
Terry Crawford ■ Eastside-Westside Monitor Coordinator
Stephen Crouch ■ Communications
John Curtin ■ Mayor's Walk/Logistics
John Davis ■ Ad Hoc
Sam Eddy ■ Teams
Phil Edmunds ■ 24-Hour Ultra Run
Warren & Patti Finke ■ Marathon Clinic
Crystal Frame ■ Volunteer Coordinator
Debbie Frank ■ Fitness Expo Coordinator
Scott Fraser ■ Course/Marathon
Susan Frohnmayer ■ 26.2 Walk
John Gardner ■ Finish Area/Entertainment
Ted Gilbert ■ Steering Committee/Announcer
Steve Gould ■ Steering Committee
Chris Hardman ■ Course Coordinator
Fred Hassel ■ Starting Line
Gayle Heffernan ■ Volunteer Coordinator
Pat Holly ■ Handicapped Athletes
Dr. Lindsey Horenblas ■ Medical Director
Dennis & Judy Ikenberry ■ Finish/Results
Alan Jensen ■ General Counsel
Wes Johns ■ Clydesdale Event
Mike Johnson ■ Special Olympics Director
Peter Kepfer ■ Aid Stations
Rebecca King ■ Walk Course/26.2 Walk
Ethan Knight ■ Director's Advisor on Youth
Sally Leben ■ Walk Start Coordinator
Donna Lee ■ Walk/Awards
Susan Leonti ■ Post-Race Party
John Lindberg ■ Packets/Registration
Bud Logan ■ Permits/Walk
Kathy McFerron ■ Ad Hoc
John McLachlan ■ S.F. Liaison
Beth Mulvihill ■ Eastside Monitor Coordinator
Laurie Mumm ■ Walk
Kiyoshi Nakamura ■ Int'l Relations Japan
Britt Lynn Nelson ■ Transportation/Kids' Run
Craig Parker ■ Logistics Coordinator
Diane Parker ■ Merchandise Coordinator
Melinda Pyrch ■ Publications
Tom Rees ■ Logistics
Tracy Richardson ■ Pasta Party
Molly Ritchey ■ Ad Hoc/Kids' Run
Steve Rickles ■ Finish Area Coordinator
Jim Schaeffer ■ Packets/Registration
Helen Smith ■ Hilton Registration
Pam Snowden, John Custer ■ 4-Wheel Drive
Greg Spahr ■ Logistics
Jeff Stacey ■ Walk/Logistics
David Steffens ■ International Runners
Wayne Stoll ■ Timing
Dale Suran ■ Treasurer
Sherry Swain ■ Design/Layout
Shirin Tavakolian ■ Start Area
Phil Todd ■ Logistics
Paul Vanture ■ Early Marathon
Dick Walker ■ Police & City Liaison
Matt Wangler ■ Teams/Tours
Dr. Craig Warden ■ Medical Coordinator
Ken Weidkamp■ Distribution
Mark Wharry ■ Five-Miler
Bob Williams ■ Clinic Coordinator
Tim Williams ■ Start Area Coordinator
Nadine Wooley ■ Director's Assistant
Fran Marrs Woolsey ■ Walk/Finish Area

Portland Marathon Committee, he has brought additional events into the race, such as the 26.2 Mile Walk. Les also added a Five-Mile Mayor's Walk and the Kids' Marafun.

Under Smith's aegis, the event grew in sophistication. He developed a full-time committee and subcommittees to work on the Marathon year-round on matters as diverse as logistics and merchandising. He proved year after year that the event could be safely run. Even with the advent of the Early Start Marathon, Les showed city officials that the unpaid Marathon staff and volunteers could protect city streets before the police arrived for the 8 A.M. race.

The facts speak for themselves. Since 1981, the number of runners participating in the Portland Marathon has taken a quantum leap from just under five hundred to over ten thousand. The Portland/Oregon Visitor's Association (POVA) has finally recognized the Portland Marathon as one of the largest yearly conventions in the city. In 1989, Road Race Management named Les Smith one of the Top Six Race Administrators in the nation, and he received the Oregon Road Runners Club Lifetime Award. In 1990, he received a merit award at *The Oregonian's* Banquet of Champions.

Volunteers on the committee had been accumulating as early as Ken Weidkamp's Island Marathon. As Ken and every other race director discovered, there were always volunteers willing to tackle any task. Ken himself is a sterling example of a valiant volunteer. Since the Marathon's beginnings almost two decades ago, he has worked on the Marathon every single year. He is still a devoted member of the official Marathon committee.

Medical aid on the Marathon course was a concern of city and race officials. But like the volunteers, medical aid has always appeared. In their earlier days, Gorman and Weidkamp used to rely on doctors who came to run the Marathon and to help in case of an emergency. During Les Smith's tenure, Emergency Room Doctor Lindsey Horenblas of St. Vincent's Hospital became active. Medical personnel were organized, and

proving receptive to the program, which exchanges runners and provides home-stays.

■Called the Grandaddy of the Five-Miler, Paul Christiansen had

the innovative idea for it in 1985. Christiansen also helped record finish line results with Jack Pessia for a number of years.

■Jim Schaeffer, a committee volunteer for more years than he is willing to acknowledge, handles the goody bag party and all Expo-day

As dawn breaks, volunteers set up finish chutes on S.W. Third Avenue.

the appropriate equipment was brought in. Dr. Horenblas still works with the Marathon, along with a two person team made up of Mamie Amundson, R.N., and Dr. Craig Warden. They are joined by 150 medical aid volunteers and half a dozen ambulances.

In 1985, Les Smith enrolled the Portland Marathon with the Association of International Marathoning (AIMS), and found people from other

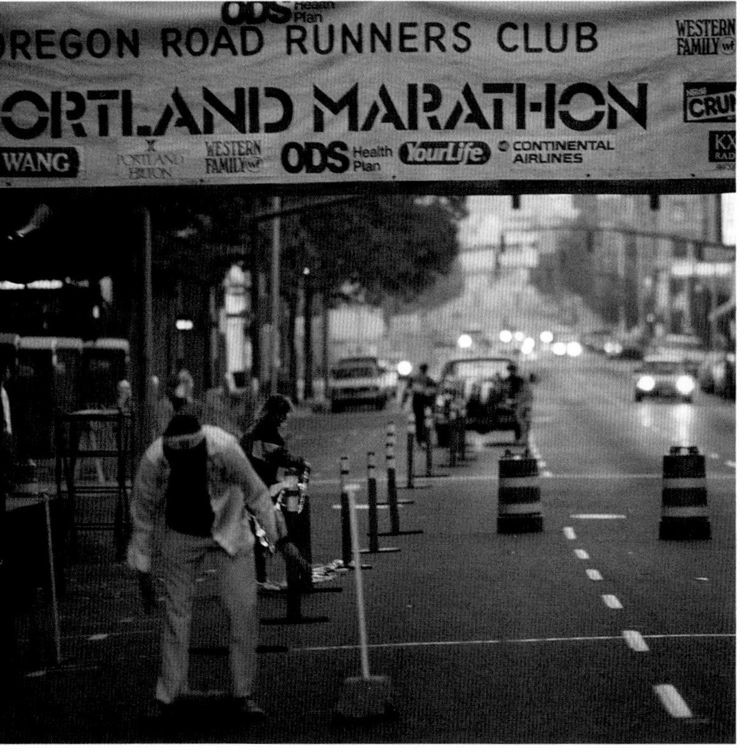

countries would travel from around the world to run in a top flight marathon. To date, runners have traveled from Europe, Central America, and the Orient to compete.

The Marathon experienced its first international faux pas in 1987 when a delegation from Japan came to run the Marathon under the misguided belief that they had an international invitation to do so. Although the Marathon Committee was nonplussed at the arrival of this formal foreign delegation, they managed to find a translator and lodgings for the group. The next year, Yoshihiro Nishimura, of Beppu, Japan, won the race in a time of 2:22:43. Now, the Japanese delegation reciprocates with an invitation to the Beppu-Oita Marathon.

Other countries have participated since publicity in the AIMS magazine began. Groups from Germany, Mexico, England, and the Soviet Union have raced here. Even the Canadians, not usually regarded as foreign travelers, have swept into town in contingents as large as three and four hundred.

logistics. He says that Expo responsibilities sometimes resemble wartime tactics and maneuvers.

■The year-round task of marathon registration belongs to capable Debbie Cook. Fortunately, handling this huge task doesn't prevent her from running for pleasure.

■**The oversized task of**

No one is left on the course alone. The last runner crosses the finish line with a motorcade, as does the first.

A big part of the polishing of the Marathon came with the computer age. A computer system to control registration seemed a pie-in-the-sky idea at first. But as the Marathon grew, monitoring finances, registration, merchandise inventory, and race results by computer became essential because it was too big a job to do by hand.

As the number of runners increased, costs kept pace. The race could not pay for itself with entry fees alone. A marathon that cost well under $1,000 in 1972 had now expanded to a budget of $280,000. And as Smith and members of the Marathon committee are quick to point out, it would cost twice as much if Portland paid prize money and appearance fees.

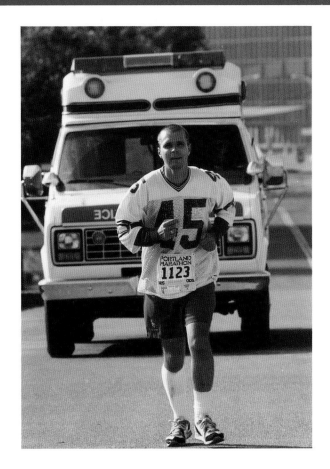

Appearance Fees and Prize Money

During the first Olympic marathon in 1896, wealthy Greek businessmen promised rewards to the Greek contender who finished in first place. A chocolate factory offered 2,000 pounds of chocolate; a barber and a tailor offered free shaves and clothes for life; Mr. Georgios Averoff, overcome with national pride, pledged his daughter's hand in marriage and a dowry of a million drachmas, which was a very tidy sum in those days.

After a long, hot, tortuous marathon, a

coordinating registration at the Expo falls to Helen Smith. For her, the back-breaking weekend is relieved only by its short tenure.

■Diane Parker fields all Marathon hotline calls and scrambles to get the merchandise booth operating at the yearly Expo.

■Race Committee members Gail Heffernan and Crystal Frame manage the enormous responsibility of training volunteers. They tell them where

Greek did win. Spyridon Louis finished first with a time of 2:58:50. He had to turn down Mr. Averoff's daughter because he was already married, but his eventual retirement from road racing should have found him well-shaved, wearing finely tailored clothes with chocolates in his pockets.

It's safe to say that Portland Marathon winners will never share the fineries bestowed upon Spyridon Louis. Portland is proud to boast a successful marathon that pays no prize money or appearance fees. But it is also safe to say that considerable citywide pride enfolds both marathoner and onlooker during the Marathon weekend.

The Portland Marathon was originally put on to the tune of less than five thousand dollars. Today, almost twenty years later, it is run for just under three hundred thousand dollars. If appearance fees and prize money were added to the equation, that amount would double. (The first place winner in the New York and Los Angeles marathons can win up to twenty thousand dollars and a new Mercedes Benz, in addition to appearance fees.) There is nothing wrong with prize money, but it is not right for Portland, Oregon.

For the first ten years of the Marathon's history, race directors anguished over how to support the Marathon. At first it was thought that the event should support itself entirely, without the help of sponsors, and at first this was a successful idea. The Marathon was able to support itself through entry fees. But as marathoning became more popular in the 1970s, the Portland Marathon felt the weight of increased responsibilities. More runners meant more aid stations, more food, more space blankets, more police and manpower on the course, more money. At one point or another, almost all the race directors concluded that more money required more sponsors, which, of course, raised the question, "How can we entice them?" The answer seemed to be big name runners, which meant paying both appearance fees and prize money. This proved to be a chicken and egg question that left the Marathon without chicken or eggs.

When Les Smith took over as race

to go, what to do, and teach them everything from how to obtain medical aid to how to hand out cups to thirsty runners.

■Marathon race-walkers have a stake in the action, as do age groups, family and corporate teams, national, and international finishers.

■**Within the**

Rehydrating the runner—a Marathon budget item that cannot be spared.

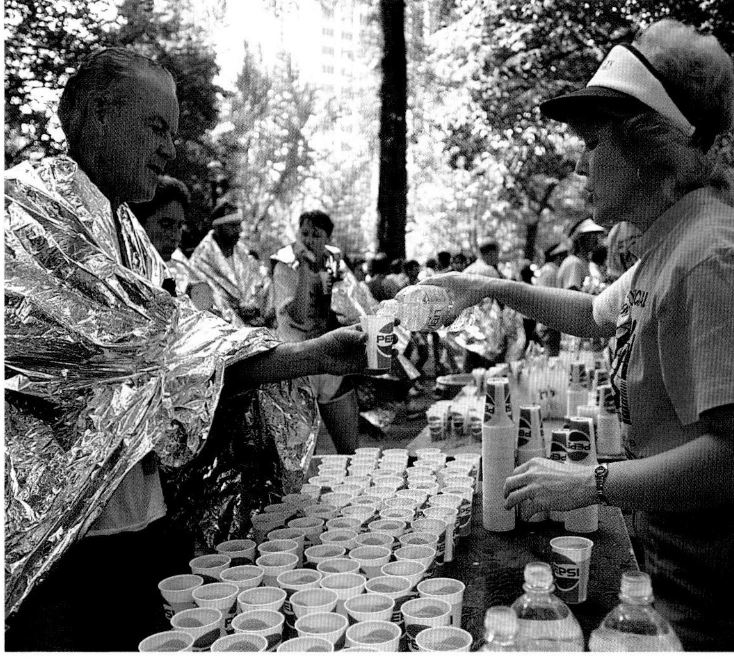

director, he decided not to agonize over the question. Instead he chose to put together a group of people to help him with the overall aspects of the Marathon. Their announced goals were to make it bigger, to make it attractive to both observer and runner, and to make it a community event.

While the Committee concentrated on accomplishing these objectives, it found sponsors interested in making the Marathon a people's event. The theme of the Portland Marathon became "Everybody is a winner." Everyone who crosses the finish line gets the TLC they deserve for their triumph. All finishers receive a medal minted at the Birmingham Mint in England and a prestigious Finisher's shirt. Women finishers also receive a rose. Age group and Division winners through tenth place receive beautiful plaques, as do First Place winners from every state in the Union and from every represented country. Sometimes, a special runner is honored with a bottle of fine Oregon wine or a Pendleton blanket.

As Les Smith says, "I am a middle-of-the-pack runner and when I finish a marathon I'm not interested in who won. I am interested in my achievement and I want something for that, be it cream to rub on my blisters or a volunteer to put a medal around my neck. My goal for the Portland Marathon has been to make everyone feel special. I want the last person crossing the finish line to feel as important as the first person and to receive the same attention." According to *Runner's World Magazine*, the Portland

Marathon's traveling mass of athletic flesh are special categories for weight lifters; slots for men over 185 pounds and women over 155 pounds; plus a pod of parents pushing baby strollers.

■The majority of Five-Milers complete the race within thirty minutes of its start.

■**David Steffens came**

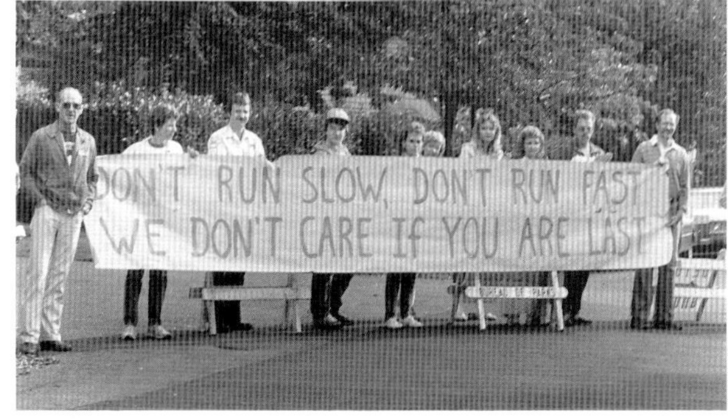

Marathon Committee has achieved that goal: "In Portland every finisher is treated like a champion. Among the marathons that celebrate everyone who goes the distance, there is none better than this Northwest Classic."

How to raise all the necessary money is the question that challenges Les Smith and the Marathon Committee throughout the year. One answer is sponsorships. Sponsors participate in the Marathon by providing cash, products, or services, and in return, they receive considerable exposure through advertising and Marathon publications. In the past, these sponsors have included Alaska Airlines, Azumano Travel, Bud Light, CMSI, Cellular One, the City of Portland, Continental Airlines, Dupont Carpet Fibers, Erv Lind Florist, First Interstate Bank, Flashback One-Hour Photo Finish, Fred Meyer, Gatorade, Hertz, Home Pride Bread, Irwin-Hodson, KEX Radio, KGW Radio and TV, KOIN-TV, KXL Radio, Miller Light, Naturite Vitamins, Nestle Crunch, Nike, ODS Health Plan, Pacific Northwest Bell, Pepsi, the Portland Bureau of Parks, Portland General Electric, the Portland Hilton, Portland Jaycees, Safeway, Security Pacific Bank, St. Vincent's Hospital and Medical Center, Thriftee Thriftway, U.S. National Bank, Wang, Western Family, Westin Benson, Weyerhaeuser, and Your Life Vitamins.

Helping Others Help Themselves

In order to obtain sponsorships, the Marathon had to prove it was doing something worthwhile for the community. The Marathon already made a strong contribution to downtown businesses by bringing people into the city, but Les Smith wanted to expand that contribution. He wanted the Marathon to give its support to people who were in need.

In 1985, the Portland Marathon Committee developed a pledge-and-run program whereby those participating in the Marathon could make a donation, based on their own performance, to a charity. The recipient for this pledge-and-run in 1985 and 1986 was a Friends of Duniway project. The project was designed to add improvements such as

in second place in the 1989 Portland Marathon but garnered first in all the local area competitions. Because a Japanese runner won the race,

Steffens was offered a trip to Japan, to run in a half marathon in Sapporo through Portland's Sister City program. Two weeks after the Portland Marthon, Steffens came in second in a field of nearly 7,000 competitors.

■Although the idea for the Clydesdale event originated in Maryland

lighting and a digital clock to the centrally located and very popular Duniway track near downtown Portland. For two years, with the help of Dennis Bromka, the Marathon helped to net close to thirty thousand dollars. The program expanded to include the installation of a soft path for runners and walkers around the upper end of the Duniway Park complex as well as other improvements to the track itself.

In 1987, with this program complete, the Marathon decided to assist two other organizations, Easter Seals and Oregon Special Olympics, as it seemed natural that the work of both organizations would appeal to runners.

Oregon Special Olympics became the designated recipient of Marathon funds through the efforts of Mike Johnson and members of the local Special Olympics chapter, who served the Marathon in a variety of ways, including

in 1987, the Portland Marathon has offered heavy weight divisions for five years. A group of local runners led by Joe Law banded together and convinced race directors to create official weight categories for the bigger runner. Participants believe that bigger is better and fondly refer to themselves as "studs" and "mares".

■Committee member Melinda Pyrch, editor of the *Oregon Distance Runner,* keeps vital Marathon statistics in front of runners' eyes.

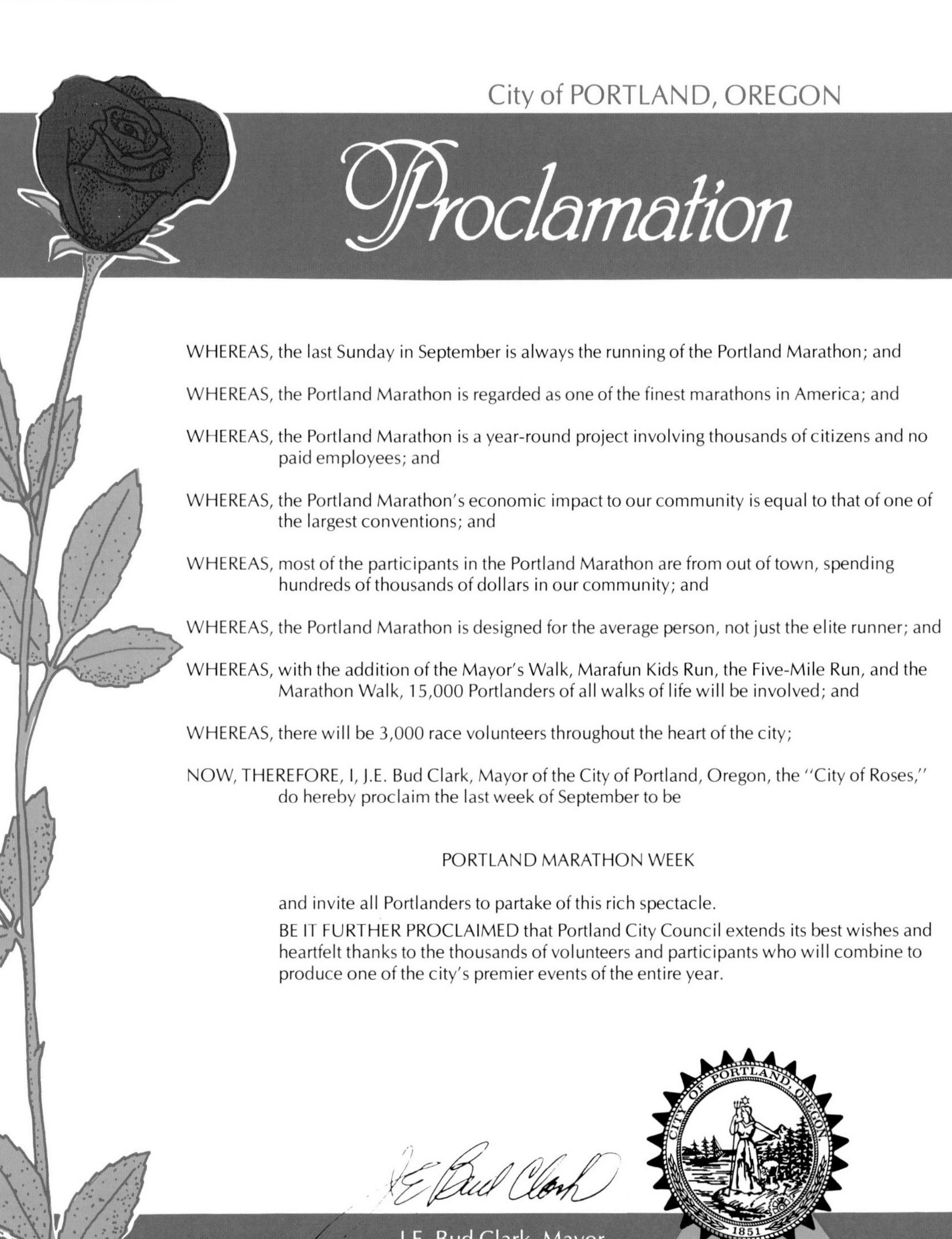

City of PORTLAND, OREGON

Proclamation

WHEREAS, the last Sunday in September is always the running of the Portland Marathon; and

WHEREAS, the Portland Marathon is regarded as one of the finest marathons in America; and

WHEREAS, the Portland Marathon is a year-round project involving thousands of citizens and no paid employees; and

WHEREAS, the Portland Marathon's economic impact to our community is equal to that of one of the largest conventions; and

WHEREAS, most of the participants in the Portland Marathon are from out of town, spending hundreds of thousands of dollars in our community; and

WHEREAS, the Portland Marathon is designed for the average person, not just the elite runner; and

WHEREAS, with the addition of the Mayor's Walk, Marafun Kids Run, the Five-Mile Run, and the Marathon Walk, 15,000 Portlanders of all walks of life will be involved; and

WHEREAS, there will be 3,000 race volunteers throughout the heart of the city;

NOW, THEREFORE, I, J.E. Bud Clark, Mayor of the City of Portland, Oregon, the "City of Roses," do hereby proclaim the last week of September to be

PORTLAND MARATHON WEEK

and invite all Portlanders to partake of this rich spectacle.

BE IT FURTHER PROCLAIMED that Portland City Council extends its best wishes and heartfelt thanks to the thousands of volunteers and participants who will combine to produce one of the city's premier events of the entire year.

J.E. Bud Clark

J.E. Bud Clark, Mayor

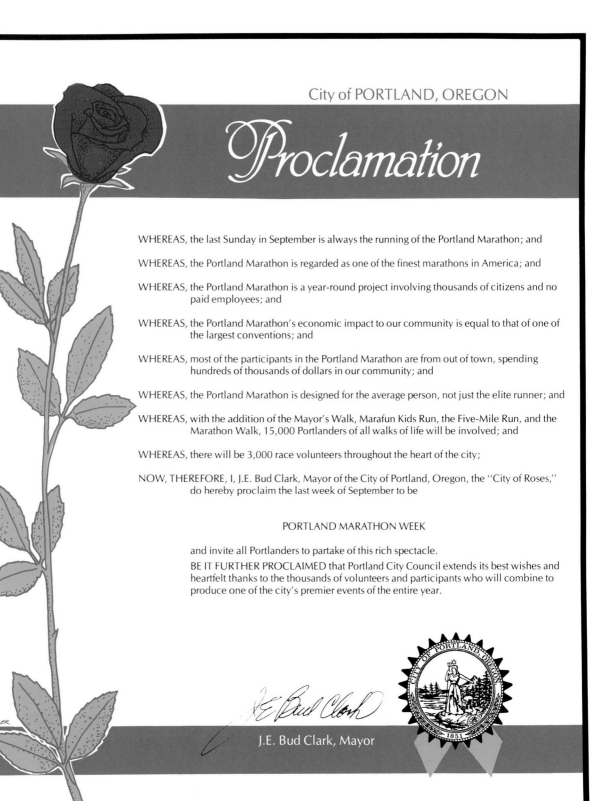

aid station and cleanup work. They had also participated in a program for Special Olympic athletes in the Five- Miler. With everyone concerned viewing fund-raising for the charities as a win/win situation, representatives of all three organizations threw themselves into the task. Sheila Owings of Easter Seals and Susan Wessinger of Oregon Special Olympics immediately began planning for a successful fund-raising campaign, including a pledge-and-run available to all Marathon participants.

In its first year, the pledge-and-run raised approximately twenty thousand dollars for the charities, which they split equally. In 1987, the program expanded. The Marathon volunteered to turn over all of its proceeds from the Pasta Party. Again, the charities went to work to make the Party a success. With the assistance of Race Committee member Jeff Clark, they helped to secure a new location, obtained food supplies from sponsors, and made requests to others in the community. The party netted several thousand dollars. As Les Smith recalls, "With the help of Special Olympics and Easter Seals we not only had a better Pasta Party with more volunteers but we also gave the charities an opportunity to make the event a fun annual occasion for their benefit."

The charities associated with the Marathon believe in a "helping others help themselves" philosophy. Easter Seals enables people with physical disabilities to live more independent lives. Local offices offer physical and psychological therapies and help with special grants and loans for therapeutic equipment. Oregon Special Olympics supports individuals who have physical or mental disabilities but still want to be athletic and compete. Every year, there are Oregon Special Olympics participants involved in the Marathon, the Five-Miler, the Mayor's Walk, the Kids' Run, and the Marathon Walk. These special athletes are an inspiration to all Marathon participants.

In 1988, the Marathon adopted a third cause, Multiple Sclerosis. The National Society supports research to find the cause and cure for M.S. and provides

■The first year the Marathon moved to its current downtown course in 1984, it experienced a 40% increase in Marathon race participants.

■The Portland/Oregon Visitors Association (POVA) recognizes the Marathon as a convention. This may seem odd, since most conventions are held

treatment and services. In 1988 and 1989, the M.S. Society assisted at a Marathon aid station and began to work with the other two charities. In 1990, Megan's Run, a 24-hour pledge and run for SIDS (Sudden Infant Death Syndrome) hooked up with the Pasta Party. Phil Edmunds spear-headed the idea and received full support from the Marathon Committee.

In keeping with its "Family Affair" philosophy, the Portland Marathon Committee has also helped the Youths at Risk (YAR) program by supporting its involvement in Marathon events. With the organization of Peggy Gallup, Youths at Risk are able to train for and participate in a citywide event. The Marathon Committee strives to help individuals as well as national charities and is happy to share the enormous publicity the Marathon generates.

Inspired by the London Marathon, the Committee has refined its goals with respect to charities. The London Marathon, the largest in the world with nearly 30,000 runners, has nearly *every* runner raising money for the Marathon's chosen beneficiaries. (Each year London chooses two charities to split the monies raised during the event.) In 1989, London Marathon runners raised nearly three million pounds through pledge-and-run activities. The Marathon donated an additional half million pounds through a fee that was charged the nearly ninety thousand runners who requested applications.

A Portland traveler who participated in the London Marathon in 1988 and was wearing a London Finisher's shirt, recalls being repeatedly asked, "How much money did you make?" Thinking these Londoners were insane to imagine he might have won prize money, he explained he was not one of the winners. Finally he realized: to Londoners, making money meant raising money for the pledge-and-run. Everyone who does is greeted as a hero.

There may be a different consciousness about fund-raising in England as a result of World War II. People recall how they teamed together to survive. The Portland Marathon Committee is

indoors, but the Marathon Convention is one of the city's biggest.

■Dennis Bromka pulls together the wild, wacky, and inspiring entertainment stations. From male belly dancers to marching bands and boom boxes, Bromka never misses a beat.

■John Gardner makes and receives Marathon

Race number still pinned to his chest, a runner finds a short nap necessary before hitting the showers.

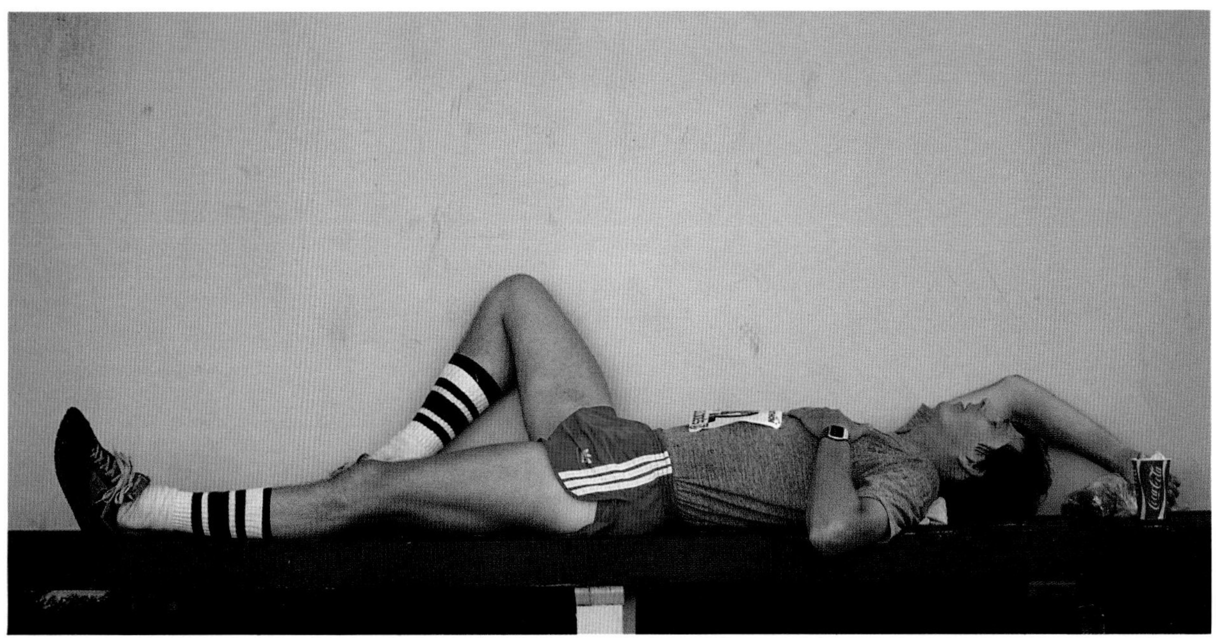

determined to raise the consciousness of participants so the Marathon's Pledge-and-Run can become as successful as London's, and every Marathon entrant can become a hero.

The history of the Marathon is not only a record of logistical misadventures and successes. Countless individual runners, many of them documented in the running notes, tell colorful tales. Brian Hermes of Minnesota asked his girlfriend to marry him at the halfway mark during the 1988 Marathon, and she accepted. (It was definitely not the fastest marathon either of them have ever run.) At the same time, Dr. Ted Hyde was running the course in his eighties. He started early, at four or five in the morning, and finished in the dogged time of eight hours. Determined, dedicated, and passionate are the words that describe Portland Marathon runners, and the thousands of enthusiastic volunteers that make this extraordinary Marathon possible each year.

calls. One long distance call came from a friend during the New York City Marathon who needed John's encouragement to finish.

■The only traffic accident in the Marathon's history involved a collision between two motorcycle policeman. Neither was harmed.

GOING THE DISTANCE

Twenty-Six Point Two

"Among the marathons that celebrate everyone who goes the distance, there is none better than this Northwest classic."

Runner's World

They jump up and down to keep warm and to shake off nerves. They laugh and chatter with their peers, form neat lines at the portable toilets, and continue to stretch and gulp down liquids. They check crowds for friends and relatives, hoping for one last hug or kiss before the gun goes off.

Others ignore the onlookers. They concentrate only on themselves. Deep in thought and serious about the immediate future, they ponder the past months of training. They adjust their shorts or tights, they pull up their socks, bend over and tie and retie their shoes, or decide on an extra shirt—especially those who have trained in Oregon weather. Their thoughts race as they complete a mental checklist. They think, "Be warm, but not too warm. Starting out a little chilled should be okay. Wearing the rain slicker may cause over-heating." Their shoes are worn but not too worn. No one ignores the experienced marathoner's advice: "Never wear brand new shoes. Make sure they are broken in. Wear good socks. You can't afford blisters. And don't forget vaseline."

Runners limber up outside of historic Portland City Hall before the race.

There is not much time left before the starter calls them to their places. Some are rubbing down with a heat rub. Others are hoping that injuries which occurred during training don't come back to haunt them. All of them have a goal to fulfill, usually more than one. The first goal, the one common goal

■Runners come decked in all kinds of garb. One year, Dennis Tong ran the entire distance dressed in a full gorilla suit and handed bananas out to the

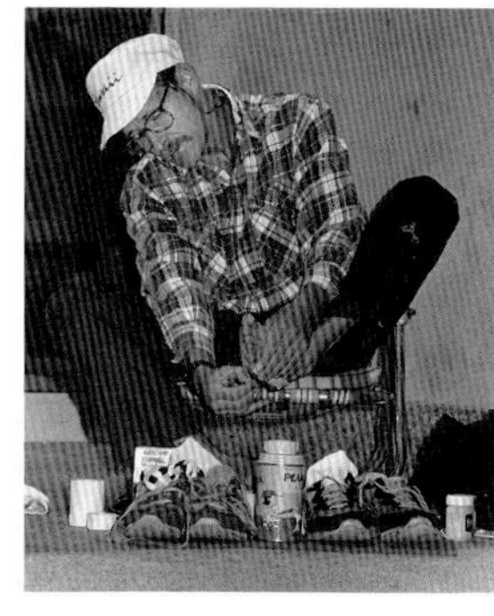

crowd. Each year, an anonymous waiter runs the Marathon in a tuxedo and white gloves while balancing a tray of Perrier and glasses.

■At the end of their

Announcer Ted Gilbert, Mayor Bud Clark, and Race Director Les Smith hail the start.

run, marathoners can feast on fruit, drinks, yogurt, and ice cream bars. The food that is not eaten is packed up and taken to Baloney Joe's, a refuge for homeless men.

■Marathon announcers achieve the remarkable goal of naming each and every runner as he or she crosses the finish line. Computers now

that every marathoner shares, is to finish. As the marathoners line up at the start line on Marathon morning, they wonder if their bodies will take them the distance. They want to finish, and this one desire blends with a myriad of other desires for race day.

One runner hopes to finish in a fast 2:45 time; another runner has an even faster time in mind; others would like to finish in four hours and be injury free at the end. The experienced marathoner also wants to complete the race injury free and, for an added bonus, he would like to shave time off his previous marathon, but a personal record (PR) for a marathoner of any caliber is not an easy goal. Ironically, as the runner becomes faster and more experienced, a PR becomes more difficult to accomplish.

A Portland runner who has run in the Marathon since 1982 explains: "I finished my first marathon, the Portland Marathon, in 4:10; my second marathon the following year in 4:00; and my third marathon five months later in 3:50. The pattern seemed great. I thought that every time I ran a marathon I would trim 10 minutes off my time. What a wrong assumption! It took me three more marathons to reach my best marathon time of 3:36:08. Twelve marathons later, I'm still trying to break 3:30." The more elite runners finishing in 2:30 or better may work years at shaving one or two minutes off their times. When they cannot make this goal, they rely on other aspirations to help them through the distance.

Marathon morning, the marathoner wonders about the personal obstacles he will need to overcome during the next few hours. He begins a private ritual to enhance his race. He checks his split times, the goal times he has set for himself at splits such as the 5, 10, and 15-mile markers. (He may note them mentally. He may have written them on his hands or wrists.) He occupies himself with a dozen small tasks designed to ease tension before the gun goes off.

His preparation began months before, when he first walked out his front door—running shoes on, watch set—and began training runs. Training

help handle a Herculean task which used to be accomplished with pins, thumbtacks, and three volunteers who went quietly or not so quietly

berserk.

■**On an average, the Portland Marathon uses 144 folding tables, 80 garbage cans, 800 plastic garbage can liners, 100**

alone, with a group, or with the Portland Marathon Training Clinics, he began to build his strengths: aerobic capacity, physical and mental endurance. He developed the best type of training program: a day of rest, some cross-training, a long run day, a short run, a middle distance, a massage, and good stretching techniques. He learned to drink quarts of water, Exceed, ERG, Gatorade, and a handful of other sports drinks and juices designed to help maintain hydration throughout the marathon distance. As well, he learned what he could or could not eat or drink prior to a long run. He learned about electrolytes, carbohydrates, and the importance of a good night's sleep. He learned intimate facts about his body and what he could demand of himself during the marathon's long ordeal.

Now months of training are focused on one morning, one run. The minutes slide away. There is only time for a prayer and a good luck wish. The marathoners throw down their drink cups, squeeze into line, and push ahead. They can't worry about shoelaces now.

They get behind the volunteer holding the sign with their estimated finish times. They feel the bodies around them, the body heat. They smell a mixture of sweat and Ben-Gay. Their arms and legs touch. They move forward. Quiet falls as the announcer yells, "One minute to start." Someone giggles, blows out air.

"Ten, nine, eight, seven." *Oh god, here we go.* "Six, five, four." *We're mov-*

garden hoses, 170 mixing pitchers, 5,000 sponges, 60,000 gallons of water, and 200,000 paper cups.

■The most common medical problem on the course is dehydration. In 1989, twenty runners required I-Vs, and ten were hospitalized. That's an unusually high number and was due to the warm temperatures.

The gun goes off, and marathoners begin their 26.2 mile voyage through the streets of Portland.

ing. "Three." *I'm going to be crushed.* "Two." *My heart's going to explode!* "One."

The gun fires. *We're off!*

Four thousand runners sweep out in a marathon tide. Feet flying, adrenalin pumping, they surge forward into the streets. The front runners are already out of sight, while those who started near the pace signs marking the 3 hour finish, the 3:30 finish, the 4 hour finish, the 4:30 finish make their way across the start line. Laughing, talking, silent, each one moves off on an individual journey they take together.

Each runner has to be concerned with the pace at which he starts the race. It is a known fact that no matter how quickly or slowly he goes, he can ruin his race by starting out too fast. He can lose his ability to finish with the flourish he would like. But adrenalin is hard to fight during the first miles, and each runner derives great pleasure in passing friends and fellow competitors during that initial surge.

The strength of his training and the rush of adrenalin may make his first mile split too fast. The runner hoping to pace himself at 6 minutes per mile will find he is running a 5:45 or 5:40. The runner hoping to run an 8 minute mile throughout the Marathon will find his first mile split is 7:15 or 7:30. Sometimes it takes from three to five miles to find the pace that will make him a comfortable runner.

Not feeling comfortable at first, not finding his pace until mile 5 or 6 or 7, isn't necessarily a bad thing. In fact, many runners and coaches believe that a runner is well-trained if he *doesn't* feel

But runners can become dehydrated even when it rains if they don't drink enough fluids.

■Marathon history is distinguished by gallantry. When a young woman from Switzerland arrived in town for the Marathon with her bicycle and back-pack, she found the youth hostel full and was out on the

The lead runners line up for a fast race. Yoshihiro Nishimura (#2), 1988 winner, feels the pressure.

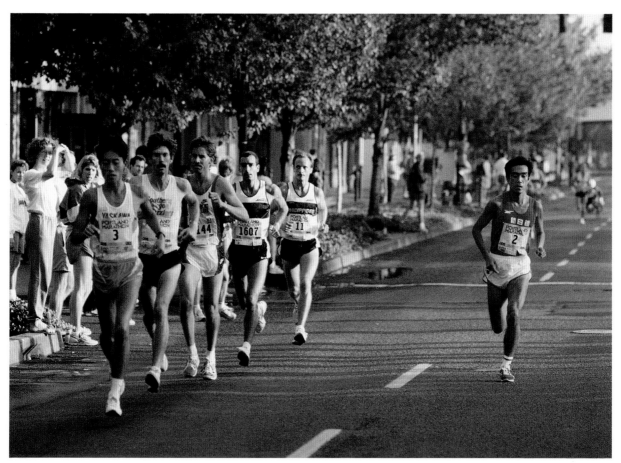

comfortable until about mile 10, because that is one sign his body has been trained for endurance. He finds his rhythm later in the course. Other runners talk about feeling *too comfortable* when they started. By mile 11, they felt terrible and knew they had to gut out another 15 miles. They would have preferred a rockier beginning. In most cases, this is a direct reflection of their training, what they ate, and even how they slept.

Once a runner calms down and finds her pace, she starts looking forward to what happens next. She starts repeating her mental checklists, she jokes with

streets until the Portland Marathon put her up in the Hilton Hotel's Mt. Hood Suite.

■The Portland Marathon goes out of its way to make runners feel good about their accomplishments. Portlander Ray Langston had run forty-nine marathons by the time he was fifty years old, and the Portland

Dragons provide entertainment as the Marathon snakes through Chinatown.

Marathon honored him with the number fifty while he ran that golden race. A year later, Masters competitor Mavis Lindgren celebrated her fiftieth marathon at age eighty-two. In honor of her achievement, she was awarded number 82.

■**In 1977, Clive Davies from Tillamook, Oregon, recorded a 60-**

her fellow runners while getting ready to make the most of the next two, three, four, or five hours. She hopes she will hear all the subtle signals her body gives her. She looks for every aid station and takes water whenever it is offered. She has learned that even though she doesn't feel thirsty at the onset, when she does start feeling thirsty she will be in trouble, so she takes water even if she doesn't really want any. Some of those runners taking drinks whether they need to or not are also looking for the portable toilets. One woman in her forties, who has been running the Portland Marathon since her early thirties, describes herself as having "a six-mile bladder." With the frankness a marathoner typically uses to describe the workings of her body during the marathon ordeal, she says, "No matter how much training I do, no matter how little or how much water I take in, I can only go six miles." That means four stops. Stopping is not too hard early in the race, but later a restroom break takes its toll. Runners find it's hard to start moving again. They sometimes begin to cramp and discover it's difficult to regain their pace.

The Portland Marathon is a dramatic course to run. When a runner starts out at 8:00 A.M., she heads straight toward Old Town, running down Fourth Avenue through the China Gate and then turning onto Marathon Avenue (a street named especially for the race), which takes her down to Front Avenue. Moving south on Front, along the Willamette River and past the crowds, the blaring music, and the entertainment stations, she runs up Harrison's quick, steep incline, and heads across the Fourth Avenue overpass. She then runs down Barbur Boulevard, passes the YMCA, where she finds her first water stop, drinks on the run, and keeps heading south until traffic cops and volunteers direct her to make a sharp hairpin left back onto well-traveled Front Avenue.

The exciting thing about this marathon loop is that a runner travels twice past her friends, the music, the noise, and the cheering crowds before heading off into the Northwest section of the

and-over Masters World Record of 2:42:22 at the Portland Marathon. No marathoner over 40 beat his record that year. Davies was 65

years old.

■Marathon photographs taken by Yukihiko Yamaoki, which have appeared in *Runner's World Magazine, The Oregon Distance*

More than a dozen aid stations provide welcome relief for thirsty runners.

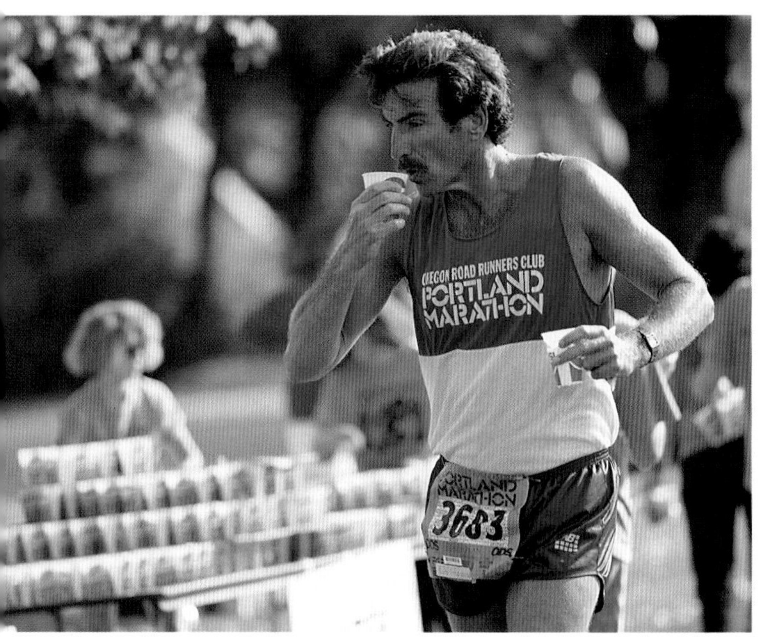

city, where she is once again met by friends, relatives, aid stations, and more entertainment. She is buoyed by the crowd's enthusiam.

When marathoners pound into Northwest Portland, they are still the only ones on the street. They trot through Northwest, around corners, over cobblestones. They moan a little, complain about the footing, and drink more water.

The first sign that they are leaving Northwest is their view of what some have called Portland's own "Heartbreak Hill." The Marathon's longest and highest hill, with an elevation of 100 feet, is nothing more than a long bridge ramp—the ramp accessing Broadway Bridge. But this "hill" lies just short of the 10-mile mark. Aches and pains are setting in. The marathoners are quieter, and the crowds have spread out.

Some of the marathoners don't think of the bridge ramp as a hill. They live in Portland, and there are hills all over the Portland metropolitan area. They don't notice this one. But other runners, from the flatlands, notice it. They see it. They dread it for the time that it takes them to get to its base and the time it takes them to get up to the top of the Broadway Bridge. They complain, "What is this? The course didn't say 'mountainous.' It said, 'Mainly flat, a few rolling hills.' They threw a mountain right in the middle of the damn race." A group of former Marines chants all the way up the ramp, "We love hills, we love hills, we love hills." They storm right up the ramp, passing complainers, and charge across the red carpet which covers the bridge. But for

Runner, the *Portland Marathon Fanfare*, and on the front cover of Warren and Patti Finke's book, *Marathoning: Start to Finish*, were photographed by Les

Smith. Yukihiko Yamaoki is Smith's nom de plume.

■A majority of Portland marathoners have a college education. One third have

They're off and running. Marathoners engulf Front Avenue.

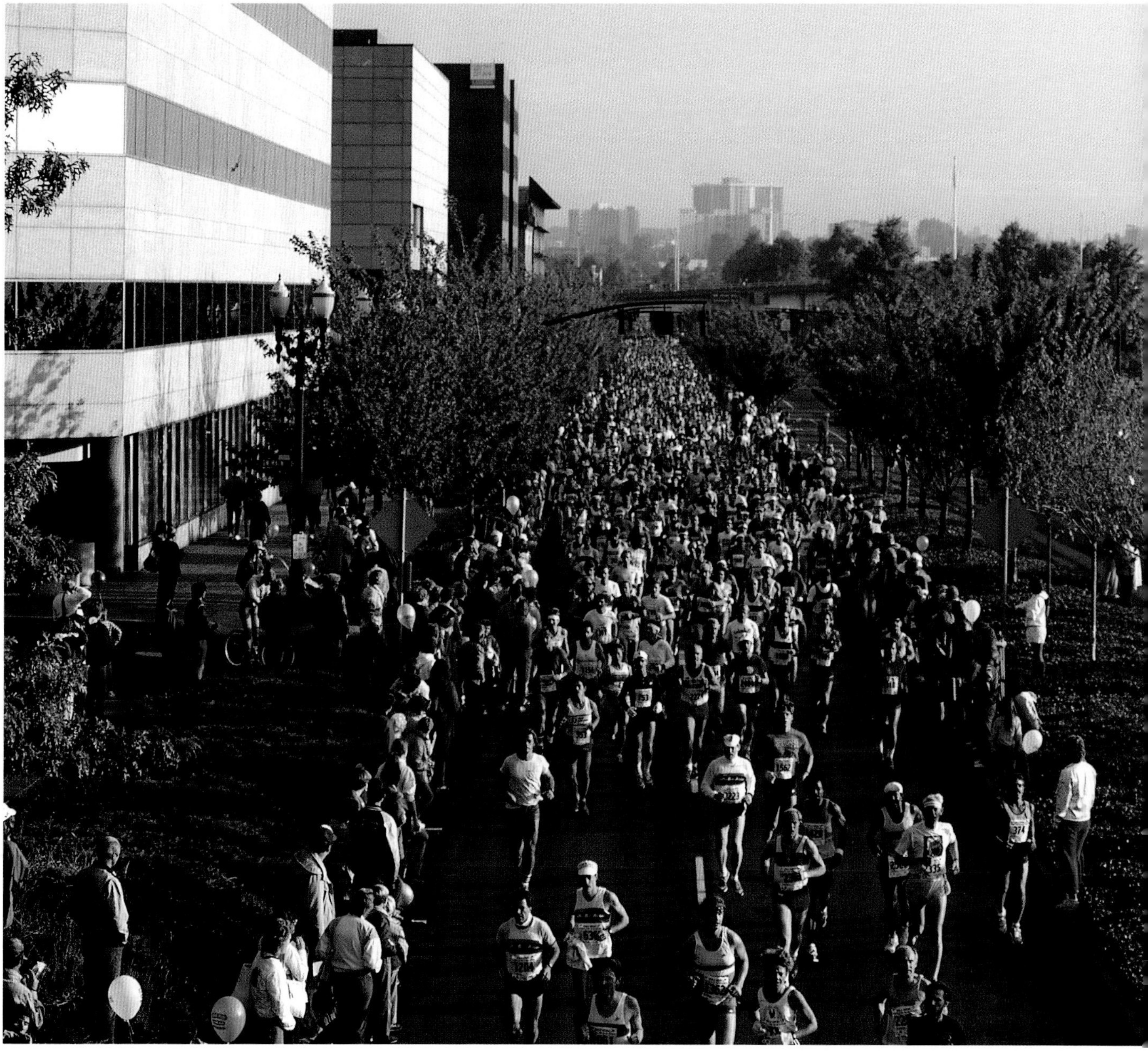

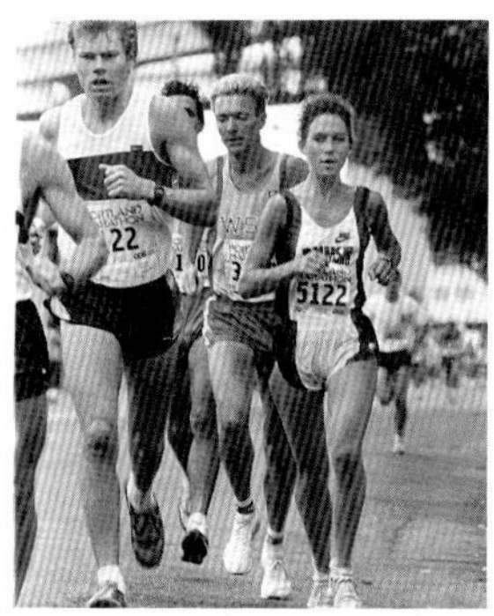

advanced degrees. Their average finish time is 3:48. Non-runners might conclude they're smart enough to know better.

■The majority of

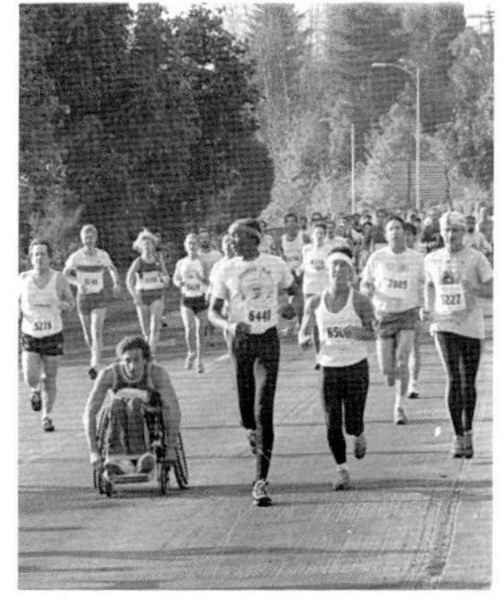

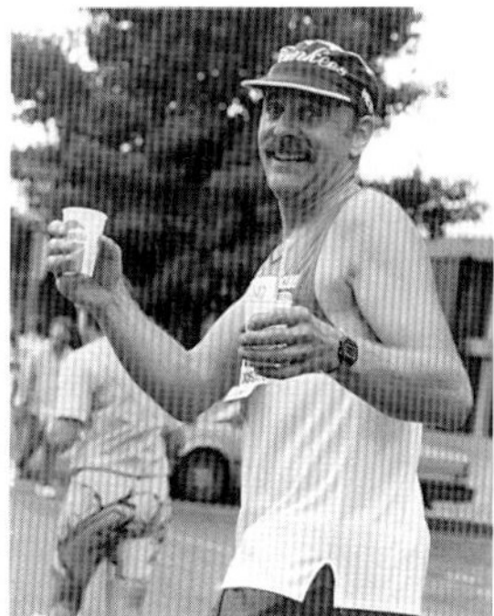

The Broadway Bridge unrolls a red carpet of welcome as runners head toward the turnaround.

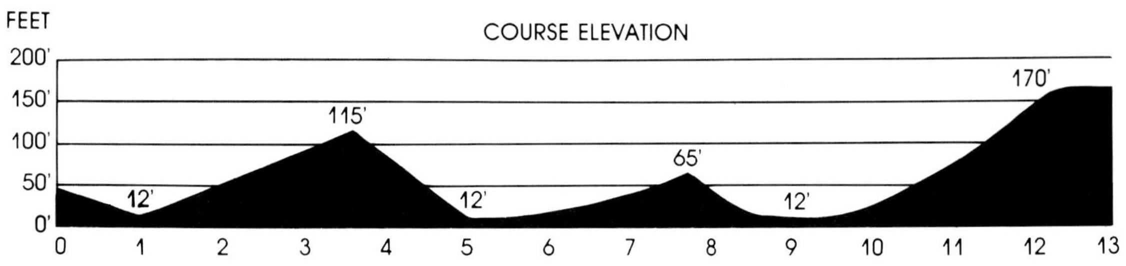

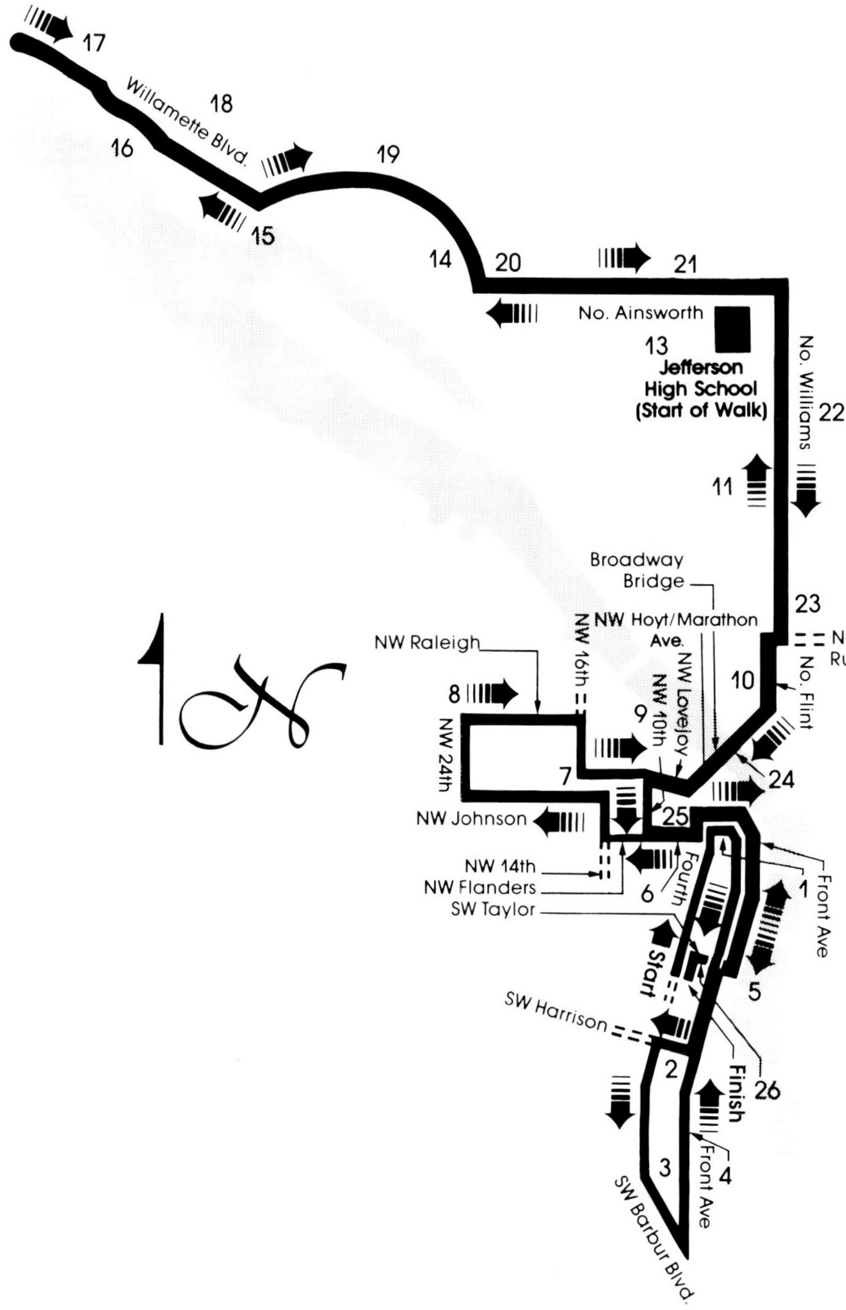

Course Map

17
Willamette Blvd.
18
16
19
15
14
20
21
No. Ainsworth
13
Jefferson High School (Start of Walk)
No. Williams
22
11
Broadway Bridge
23
NW Hoyt/Marathon Ave.
No. Russell
NW Raleigh
NW 16th
NW Lovejoy
NW 10th
10
No. Flint
8
9
NW 24th
7
24
NW Johnson
25
NW 14th
NW Flanders
SW Taylor
Fourth
6
1
Front Ave
Start
5
SW Harrison
2
Finish
26
3
4
Front Ave
SW Barbur Blvd.
N

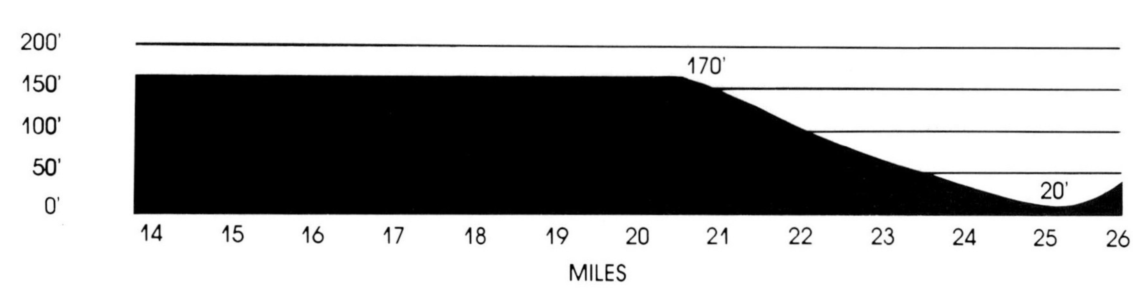

Heading home, racers pass their friends after the turn-around.

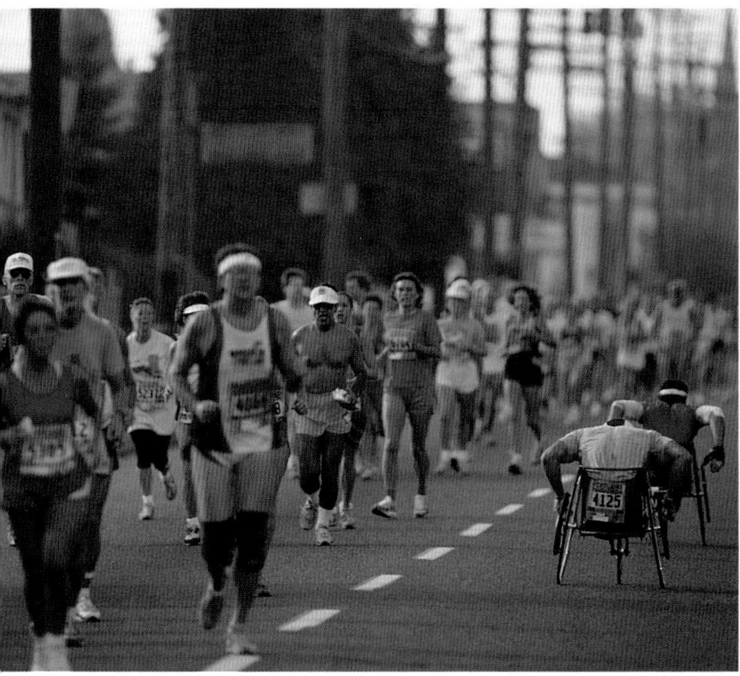

many, chanting and training do not help them on their way to the top. It is the huge aid station that looms beyond the crest of the ramp like an oasis that pulls these runners up and onward.

The elite runners who make it to the bridge and race across the carpet laid over the steel gridwork do not meet any of the walkers coming back into town, but they may be passing the wheelchair athletes who left the start line a minute ahead of them. The majority of the runners crossing the Broadway Bridge begin meeting the Five-Mile Mayor's walkers. These walkers yell merrily to the runners, "Good job! Great going! Halfway there almost," while the runners pass by waving and smiling, calling, "Great job, walkers!" In 1987, it was reported that a group of five or six marathoners sang to the walkers as they ran, "There he was just a walking down the street, singing *Do-wah-Diddy Diddy dum-Diddy-down*."

Four miles after crossing the Willamette River, traveling down Williams Avenue and turning onto Ainsworth, the marathoner reaches the halfway mark. It is here that he may find himself out on his own. It is around this point in time that he often loses the partner with whom he has been running. Paces have slowed or picked up. The marathoner starts concentrating more on himself. He is thinking about the turnaround near mile 17, and that is probably all he is thinking about. The turnaround looms ahead. Psychologically, it seems like the halfway mark. Mile 13, which should have climactic pull as the halfway point, is anticlimactic. The only

Portland marathoners are 35 to 39 years old. The next largest age group is 30 to 34, followed by 40 to 44. One might well ask where the younger

generation is, but marathoners typically come into their own at age 30.

■**Of Portland's marathon field, 10% are CEOs,**

thing it has going for it is a couple of portable toilets and a few people standing on a corner.

As the slower runner heads down Ainsworth Boulevard toward Willamette Boulevard, he begins to meet the runners who have been surging in front of him, who went out first and are still in the lead. These are the top one hundred men, five to ten top women, and the fastest wheelchair athletes who have made the turnaround and are heading back downtown to the finish line, while he heads toward the turnaround. He also starts to encounter stragglers, runners whose hamstrings tightened, whose knees gave out, who just could not make it. Meanwhile, he is trying to shake off his own pain. He wants to hold out, but his feet are hot, or he has developed a bad blister, or the muscles in his back have cramped. This is when almost every runner wonders why he decided to run a marathon.

But as he gets closer to the north end of Willamette Boulevard and the turnaround, the running crowd gets bigger, and he can't wait to get there and go home with it. Suddenly he forgets his bothersome knees or ankles or the arms that won't shake out. He finds friends in the crowd running toward the turnaround or running toward home. Everyone looks for friends, for relatives. They cheer each other on. They encourage runners who have obviously

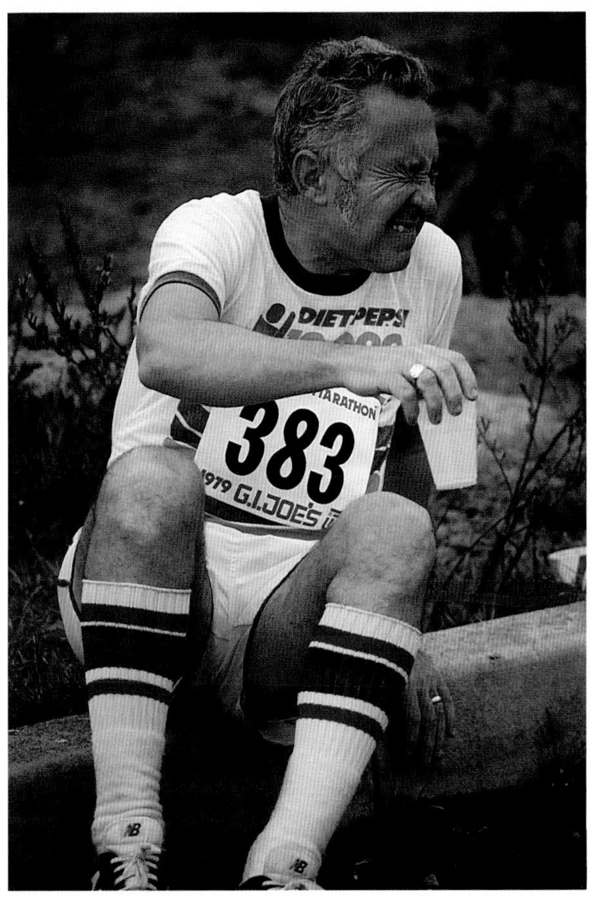

Hitting the wall, or at least the curb, a marathoner takes a break.

administrators, and managers. Their average time is 3:45:45. Their closest competitors, number wise, are teachers, professors, and

instructors with 8% of the field and average finish times of 3:50:23. Farmers, .04% of the field, have some the fastest times with an average of 3:29.

injured a muscle, runners limping along but still going toward the finish line. Although the fall-out rate in Portland is not great, approximately 2 percent of the runners who have entered will be forced to quit. Medical crews, ambulances, and committee staff riding on bikes immediately help all the runners who are forced to retire.

There is exhilaration but there may also be intense irritation. This is the time when the weather or any other element of the race can really bother a runner. This is when he gets grumpy, even with the volunteers cheerfully handing out glasses of water. He wonders why the volunteers stand so far out in the street, why they have Exceed and not water, or why water and not Exceed. He wonders why it is just now that the sweat starts to run down his face and into his eyes. One runner likes to run in the heat. Another prefers rain. Still others like a wind at their backs. Others want a completely calm day. Something is always wrong for someone. No wind, too much wind, no rain, rain, no sunshine. This is when the marathoner starts to complain.

The sweat on underarms has turned into salt and is chafing the edges of shirts. Men are wondering why they didn't band-aid their nipples—they're bleeding. Women are wondering why they didn't cut their hair shorter—their heads are sweaty, itchy. If it is raining, the weight of their shoes is annoying them, and they are getting blisters. If the wind has been at their back as they

Waiters and waitresses, .03% of the total, zip in at 3:38. ■Race director Les Smith, challenged to run fifty marathons by his fiftieth birthday, traveled to Europe to run the last two in Rotterdam and Paris. He ran these marathons three weeks apart and threw in two half marathons in Belgium in between.

Fifteen miles into the race, the turnaround's centrifugal force sends runners spinning home.

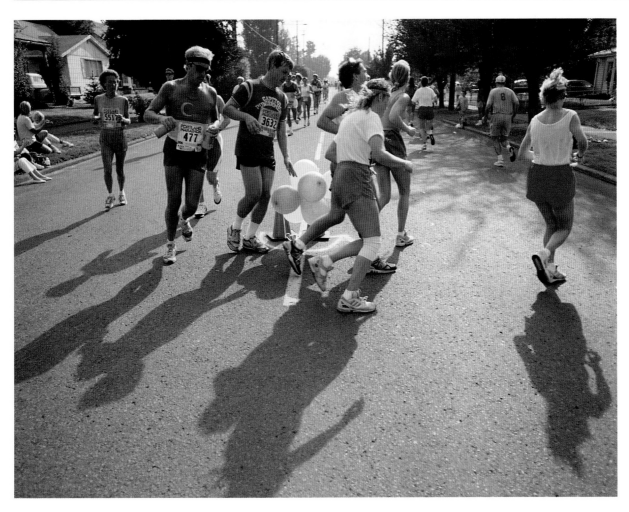

go down Willamette, the turnaround looming ahead is not going to bring them any good luck. It is going to bring the wind right into their faces.

But when the runner reaches the turnaround, there is jubilation. He now has two and a half miles to put a smile on his face. Flashback Photo has set up its camera at mile 20, ready to shoot anyone wearing a little ribbon pinned to his race shirt. It is amazing that after 20 miles of physical calamities a runner

Due to exceptional European cuisine, he also gained 13 pounds, slowing his finish times by 22 minutes.

■Dr. George Sheehan writes, "Statistics on sexual activity suggest that actual energy expenditure is in the order of a 50-yard sprint." This implies that sex the night before a marathon will

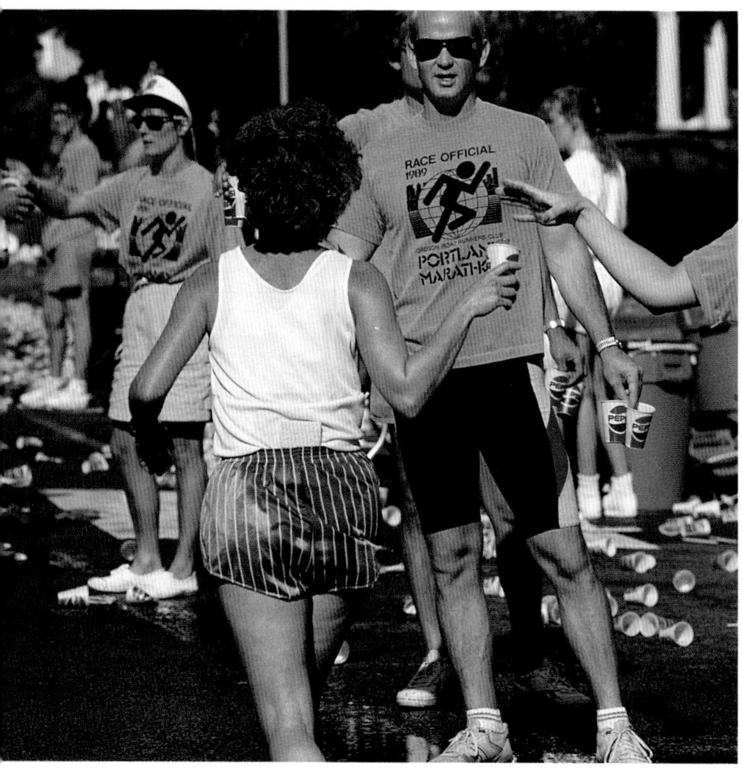

During a hot Marathon, water is plentiful, and sponges are hoarded.

is still able to summon up a smile, do something funny, wave at the camera. One year, an Englishman, Peter Torre, arrived at the Flashback post and told its crew to stand together and say cheese. Then he whipped out his camera, which he had carried the entire distance, and took their picture.

When the Flashback point is reached, the marathoner turns left and heads again onto Ainsworth. She is heading back toward the city, toward the Broadway Bridge, finishing the last 10K of the race. This is the moment when the marathoner adjusts her thinking. She has been running miles: one mile, two miles, three miles, four miles, clicking them off all the way to mile 20 at Flashback. Now she thinks, "All I have left is a 10K." To a nonrunner, this may seem like a mathematically crazy way to count, but to the runner who has participated in many 10Ks, as most marathoners have, this is the only way to count psychologically. Most mara-thoners have run one or two or more 20-mile runs, and many marathoners have run in a 10K. So to run 20 miles and then run a 10K seems physically possible, while to run 26.2 miles presents a whole different set of psychological roadblocks for a runner who needs no other demands at this point in the race.

All marathoners want to traverse only 26.2 miles and not a foot more. They have learned that if they don't run efficiently, paying attention to the turns on the course, they can pick up

not impact a runner's finish time.

■Dr. Stephen Weil of Lake Oswego, marathoner and sports physician, with an average 2:40 finish time

additional mileage. But they must also watch how they run. If they can keep their lateral and vertical movements to a minimum, they will run just 26.2 miles. If they don't, they may run hundreds of yards, even miles farther.

The New York Times reports that ". . . runners do not run in a straight line. Every runner moves laterally and vertically as he runs. At first glance, this sideways and up-and-down movement doesn't seem like much, but once you measure those extraneous movements in slow-motion and multiply them by the number of strides in a race, it soon becomes evident that every runner runs much farther than required.

"A runner takes approximately 1,000 strides per mile. This means that every error, no matter how small, is magnified 1,000 times during a marathon." However, a time comes when marathoners no longer care about the number of times their feet hit the pavement and they cannot concentrate on their running style. They are simply trying to endure.

All along the course, entertainment stations have regaled the runner every one or two miles, and as he moves down Ainsworth, tired, aching, hot, he reaches more entertainment: cheerleaders, male belly dancers, blasting stereos, along with water and food. The runner really appreciates it. Every aid and entertainment station, every piece of goodwill given from the sidelines, helps to pick up his pace a little bit, helps him go another few feet, another few miles.

Finally the marathoner turns off Ainsworth and gets back on Williams Avenue. He can see a giant, colorful hot-air balloon rising up ahead, near the next aid station. The aid stations seem

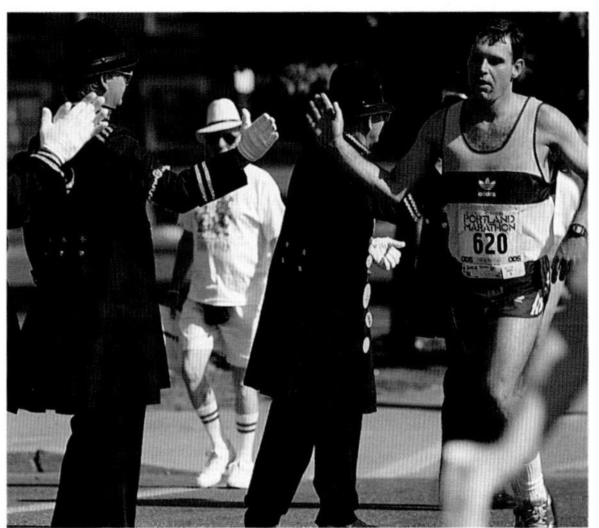

Keystone Cops give high-fives and point out short-cuts to weary runners.

in the Portland Marathon, says, "My training this year has been intense. As usual, my longest training run will be last year's marathon."

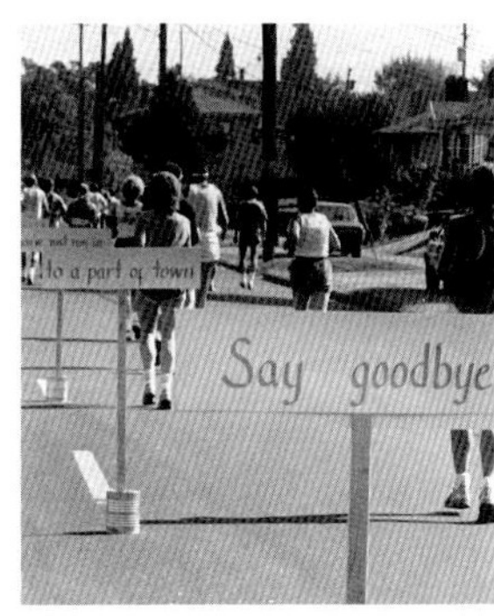

■In his book, *Galloway's Book on Running*, Jeff recommends a two-month-long race break after a marathon to allow the body to fully

The key is determination. It is a fact that more runners complete five marathons than complete just one.

recover.

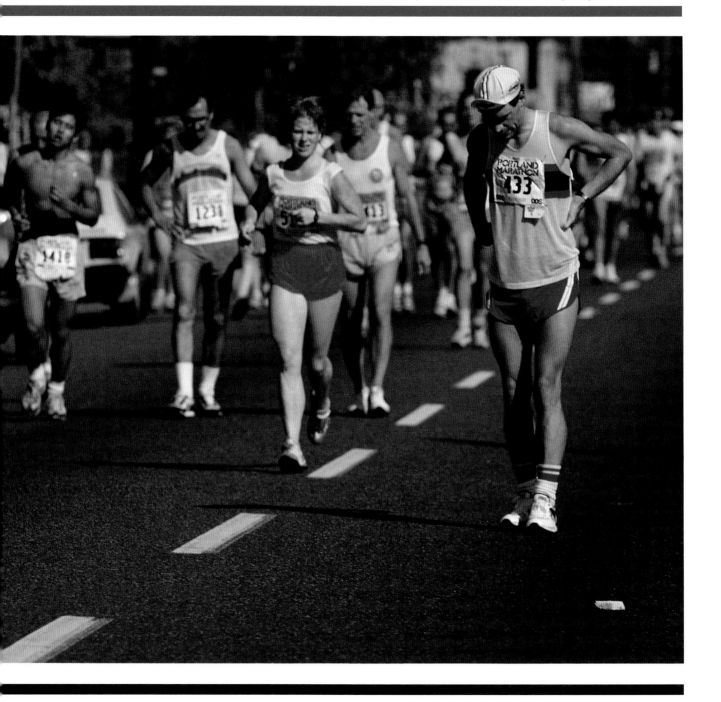

■Hugh Mount says, "The best advice I can give to the novice marathoner is to carry money—you never know if you might need a cab, a coke, or a cup of coffee. At the New York Marathon, I stopped at a bar with a fellow runner and bought a beer before finishing the race."

■Average temperatures at the Portland Marathon range from 52-54 degrees at the start to 58 degrees at the finish.

■Leonard Hill has won

to be getting farther and farther apart, but this is a function of his increasing exhaustion, not actual fact. Now he passes a hospital complex and thinks about how much closer he is to the red-carpeted Broadway Bridge. Runners have likened the bridge to the yellow brick road, a mental uplift, welcoming marathoners back to downtown Portland. At the end of the carpet is the large, 24-mile marker and one of the largest, longest, biggest aid stations. It is a favorite because once a marathoner reaches it, there are only two miles left and he can get a cup of water and roll down the hill. And down he goes, left down the Tenth Avenue ramp, hanging another left onto Flanders Street.

One of the finest things about the Portland Marathon is its second-half, negative split. This means that the last thirteen miles are faster than the first thirteen. The reason is that after mile 13 the course is level, then starts to go downhill. The marathoner has a long, pleasant downhill after mile 22. The last 10K is very quick, and it reflects in times. Now the front runners and the middle of the marathon pack pour off the Tenth Avenue bridge ramp. They are still going strong and they can't wait to cross the finish line.

It is a different story for the four and five-hour-plus runners in the rear. This is where people are straggling, struggling to make ends meet, hoping their bodies will endure. They run, they walk. They run, walk, crawl. They do whatever

A woman springs toward the finish. Doctors say women may have more stamina for marathoning than men.

the Marathon four times, once with enough lead time to eat breakfast before his closest competitor crossed the finish line. Susan Rossiter won the

first Marathon, setting a world record for her age group. Ten years later, she won again under her married name of Sue Henderson.

■**When Clive Davies**

they can to finish. These marathoners cheer each other on. Nobody snubs a slow or injured runner. They all cheer at him to keep on going.

When the runner leaves the bridge, he goes back through Old Town, makes another trip down Marathon Avenue, and heads back onto Front Avenue. When he reaches Front, he begins to count the blocks to the finish, which still seems far away. Runners say that it doesn't matter that the onlookers are cheering them on. When they tell the runner he has only three blocks left to go as he forces his body down Front Avenue and onto Salmon, they could be telling him he has three more miles or thirty. It doesn't compute. It doesn't quite click.

A woman runner recalls how she came down Front and began to think that everyone running the race was shorter than she was. Her body was at the end of its resources. She had begun to hallucinate. This is often associated with hitting the wall, a phrase that describes running out of energy supplies. Hitting the wall usually happens between the 18 and 20 mile marks. When a runner hits the wall, it is very difficult to turn things around. It is the lucky runner who hits the wall and begins to hallucinate during the final three blocks of the race.

While it is true that the Portland Marathon has a negative split and that it is level and downhill from the turnaround, there are two blocks with a small upgrade at the end. After 26 miles, with only 385 yards to go, it seems like a very bad trick played by the gods. Somehow, the runner makes it up the incline on Salmon which seems twice as high as

broke his first Masters Marathon World Record at age sixty, it wasn't the fast time that everyone talked about. It was his experimental breakfast of a large meal of pancakes just two hours prior to the race.

■Most runners think that if they can run three miles, they can run a 10K (6.2 miles). If

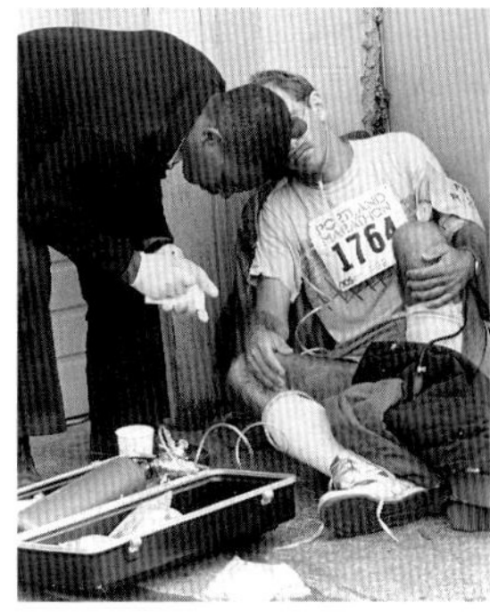

the Broadway Bridge, and hangs a left on Third Avenue. Her body is at the end of its resources. It is running only because her mind is forcing it to run. And there, like a gift from the gods, are the finish chutes. The finish line. The smiling, cheering, clapping crowds. The runner hears her name announced by Ted Gilbert, the Marathon's faithful announcer. He tells the runner if she made a PR. He tells her time, tells the crowd her age and the name of her state or country.

It is this audible encouragement that lets the runner tap her last morsel of energy and sprint forward, looking as good as she can. She may also be trying to pick off one more runner, to get in just a little faster than somebody else. Then, finally, almost surprisingly, it's over. She crosses the finish line.

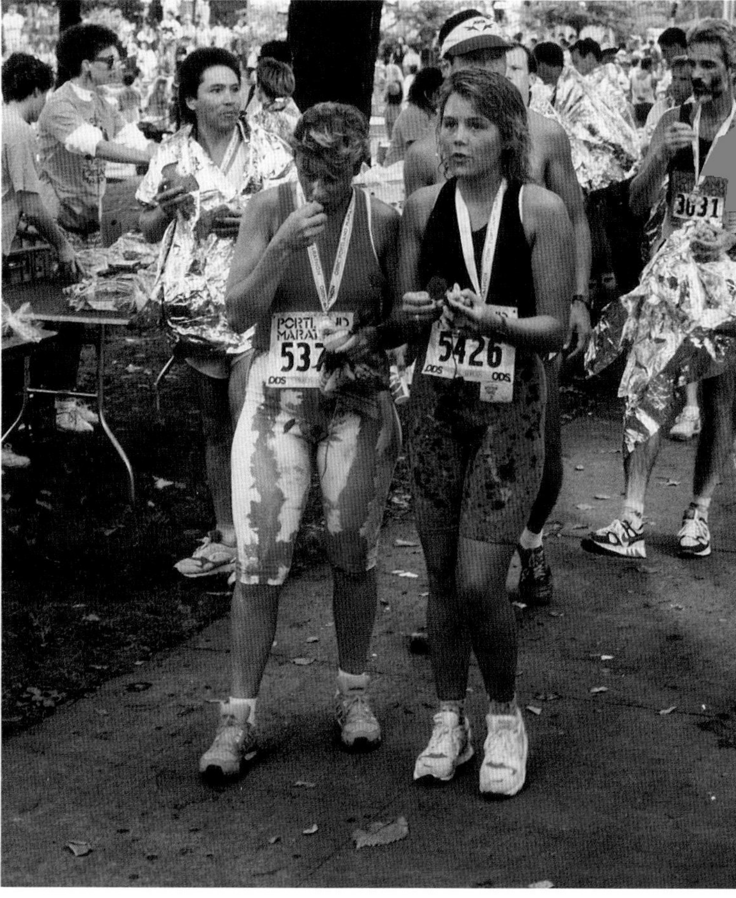

In this environment, a drink with a friend takes on new meaning.

Roses appear, a medal, a space blanket. She is personally escorted by one of the many volunteers at the finish line until the volunteer is certain that she can take care of herself, get her own juice, water, refreshments. If the volunteer doesn't think she can, she is taken to the medical aid station or to the massage table, if requested, where she gets the attention she needs before leaving the enclosed finish area.

The finish area is for runners only. This is where they are pampered and find solace after their run. Directly

they can run five miles, they can run a 15K (9.3 miles). This optimism begins to break down before the great wall of the marathon.

■**In 1989, three generations of the Nichols family and Nichols relatives entered the marathon, including the Nichols family, the Gustafson family, and the Hartley**

Finishers eagerly hunt for their names and times on the results board.

This is where they are pampered and find solace after their run. Directly across the street from the finish area is the Portland Building, housing the prestigious Finisher's T-shirts. First the runners have taken in refreshments, received a massage or whatever else was necessary, maybe just a nap in the grass, then they go across the street and pick up their shirts. Then they walk back into the finish area to look at the results that are being posted. They look for their name and time, find it, and are satisfied. It has been recorded for history that they completed the Marathon. Their times are recorded as testimony to that fact. They have gone the distance.

family, eight in all. They say they go everywhere. Their motto is "Have car, will race."

■In 1989, Debra Myra took first place overall, first place in her age division, first place in the Northwest competition, and first place for a local area runner.

■**Ken Weidkamp,**

Going the distance leaves a runner triumphant and tired.

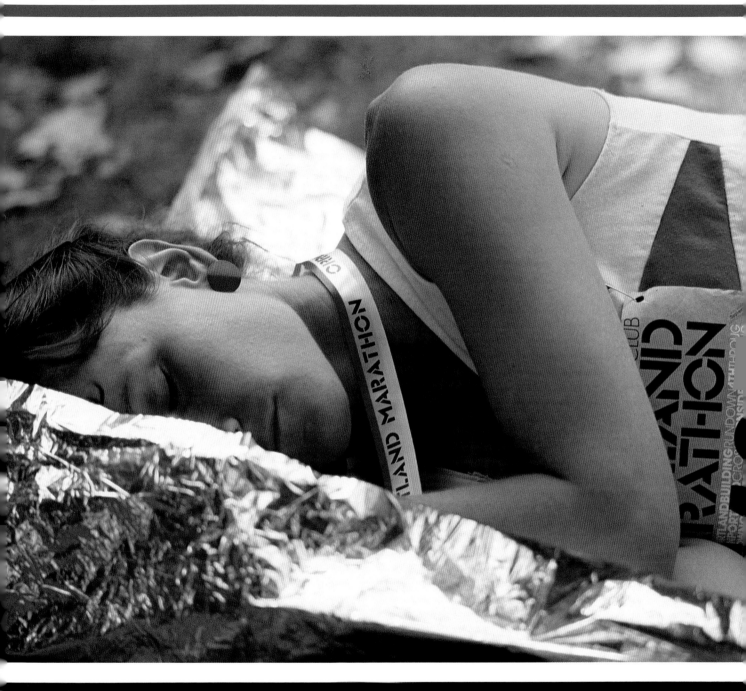

Portland's first race director, was frightened into running. At the age of 37, a close friend died, and Weidkamp realized he was almost

as big as a whale, had no dietary discipline, and no exercise program. He began to jog and before long he had lost 40 pounds and completed a marathon.

Portland Marathon Course Pace Chart

Estimated Finish Times		2:15	2:30	2:45	3:00	3:15	3:30	Comments
Miles	1.0	5:04	5:31	6:12	6:45	7:19	7:53	Uphill on Front Avenue
	2.0	10:19	11:15	12:37	13:45	14:54	16:03	Steep uphill on Harrison
	3.0	15:41	17:06	19:11	20:55	22:40	24:25	Downhill Front Avenue
	4.0	20:49	22:41	25:26	27:45	30:04	32:23	Slightly downhill
	5.0	25:48	28:07	31:32	34:24	37:16	40:08	Flanders St. slightly uphill
	6.0	30:52	33:38	37:44	41:10	44:36	48:01	Uphill Johnson Street
	7.0	36:06	39:20	44:07	48:08	52:08	56:09	Downhill 24th Avenue
	8.0	41:16	44:59	50:27	55:02	59:37	1:04:13	Downhill on Raleigh
	9.0	46:27	50:37	56:46	1:01:56	1:07:05	1:12:15	Uphill to Broadway Bridge
	10.0	51:47	56:26	1:03:17	1:09:03	1:14:48	1:20:33	Uphill on Williams Ave.
	11.0	57:07	1:02:15	1:09:49	1:16:10	1:22:30	1:28:51	Still on Williams
	12.0	1:02:16	1:07:51	1:16:06	1:23:01	1:29:56	1:36:51	Flat on Ainsworth
	13.0	1:07:24	1:13:28	1:22:23	1:29:53	1:37:22	1:44:51	Flat on Willamette Blvd.
	14.0	1:12:33	1:19:04	1:28:40	1:36:44	1:44:48	1:52:52	University of Portland
	15.0	1:17:42	1:24:40	1:34:58	1:43:36	1:52:14	2:00:52	Keep running
	16.0	1:22:50	1:30:17	1:41:15	1:50:27	1:59:40	2:08:52	Turnaround 16.75 miles
	17.0	1:27:59	1:35:53	1:47:32	1:57:19	2:07:05	2:16:52	Flat on Willamette Blvd.
	18.0	1:33:08	1:41:29	1:53:50	2:04:10	2:14:31	2:24:52	More of the same
	19.0	1:38:16	1:47:06	2:00:07	2:11:02	2:21:57	2:32:52	Still more
	20.0	1:43:25	1:52:42	2:06:24	2:17:54	2:29:23	2:40:53	Smile for photo
	21.0	1:48:34	1:58:19	2:12:41	2:24:45	2:36:49	2:48:53	Downhill on Williams
	22.0	1:53:42	2:03:55	2:18:59	2:31:37	2:44:15	2:56:53	Good downhill
	23.0	1:58:42	2:09:21	2:25:05	2:38:16	2:51:27	3:04:39	Broadway Bridge again
	24.0	2:03:41	2:14:48	2:31:11	2:44:55	2:58:40	3:12:24	Down 10th Street ramp
	25.0	2:08:44	2:20:18	2:37:21	2:51:39	3:05:58	3:20:16	Mar. Ave./to Front Ave.
	26.0	2:13:56	2:25:58	2:43:42	2:58:35	3:13:28	3:28:21	Quick Uphill on Salmon
	26.2	2:14:59	2:27:07	2:44:59	2:59:59	3:14:59	3:29:59	Finish line on Third Ave.

Estimated Finish Times		3:45	4:00	4:15	4:30	4:45	5:00	Comments
Miles	1.0	8:27	9:01	9:35	10:08	10:42	11:16	Uphill on Front Avenue
	2.0	17:12	18:21	19:29	20:38	21:47	22:56	Steep uphill on Harrison
	3.0	26:09	27:54	29:39	31:23	33:08	34:53	Downhill Front Avenue
	4.0	34:41	37:00	39:19	41:38	43:57	46:15	Slightly downhill
	5.0	43:00	45:53	48:45	51:37	54:29	57:21	Flanders St. slightly uphill
	6.0	51:27	54:53	58:19	1:01:45	1:05:11	1:08:36	Uphill Johnson Street
	7.0	1:00:10	1:04:10	1:08:11	1:12:12	1:16:13	1:20:13	Downhill 24th Avenue
	8.0	1:08:48	1:13:23	1:17:58	1:22:33	1:27:09	1:31:44	Downhill on Raleigh
	9.0	1:17:25	1:22:34	1:27:44	1:32:54	1:38:03	1:43:13	Uphill to Broadway Bridge
	10.0	1:26:18	1:32:04	1:37:49	1:43:34	1:49:19	1:55:05	Uphill on Williams Ave.
	11.0	1:35:12	1:41:33	1:47:54	1:54:15	2:00:35	2:06:56	Still on Williams
	12.0	1:43:46	1:50:42	1:57:37	2:04:32	2:11:27	2:18:22	Flat on Ainsworth
	13.0	1:52:21	1:59:50	2:07:20	2:14:49	2:22:19	2:29:48	Flat on Willamette Blvd.
	14.0	2:00:55	2:08:59	2:17:03	2:25:07	2:33:10	2:41:14	University of Portland
	15.0	2:09:30	2:18:08	2:26:46	2:35:24	2:44:02	2:52:40	Keep running
	16.0	2:18:04	2:27:17	2:36:29	2:45:41	2:54:54	3:04:06	Turnaround 16.75 miles
	17.0	2:26:39	2:36:25	2:46:12	2:55:59	3:05:45	3:15:32	Flat on Willamette Blvd.
	18.0	2:35:13	2:45:34	2:55:55	3:06:16	3:16:37	3:26:58	More of the same
	19.0	2:43:48	2:54:43	3:05:38	3:16:33	3:27:28	3:38:24	Still more
	20.0	2:52:22	3:03:52	3:15:21	3:26:51	3:38:20	3:49:50	Smile for photo
	21.0	3:00:56	3:13:00	3:25:04	3:37:08	3:49:12	4:01:15	Downhill on Williams
	22.0	3:09:31	3:22:09	3:34:47	3:47:25	4:00:03	4:12:41	Good downhill
	23.0	3:17:50	3:31:01	3:44:13	3:57:24	4:10:35	4:23:47	Broadway Bridge again
	24.0	3:26:09	3:39:54	3:53:38	4:07:23	4:21:08	4:34:52	Down 10th Street ramp
	25.0	3:34:34	3:48:53	4:03:11	4:17:29	4:31:48	4:46:06	Mar. Ave./to Front Ave.
	26.0	3:43:14	3:58:07	4:13:00	4:27:53	4:42:46	4:57:39	Quick Uphill on Salmon
	26.2	3:44:59	3:59:59	4:14:59	4:29:59	4:44:59	4:59:59	Finish line on Third Ave.

Courtesy of Patti and Warren Finke, wY'east Consulting.

After they find their time, marathoners take their weary legs home.

■The two fastest Portland Marathon times were logged within three seconds of each other. Monte Brothwell ran the Memorial Coliseum course in 2:17:50, and Alan Knoop ran the current downtown course in 2:17:53.

■The two fastest women's times are separated by just thirty

Running a marathon requires commitment. Commitment to running and commitment to learning. Runners might well be advised to learn the following:

■ The main energy supplies used in endurance running are carbohydrates (stored in the body as glycogen) and fat. These are broken down in the presence of oxygen in a process called aerobic metabolism.

■ As stores are depleted, glycogen breaks down further into pyruvate and, lacking oxygen, into lactic acid.

■ The body can endure only limited amounts of lactic acid.

■The body cannot store enough glycogen for the duration of the marathon.

■ Many marathoners experience a severe energy loss around the 20-mile point. This is called "Hitting the Wall."

■ The physiologic goals of a marathon training program are to optimize aerobic metabolism—to metabolize fat better and store more glycogen.

■ Training improves cardiovascular and respiratory systems. The heart muscle increases in size and weight, and the amount of blood increases.

■ One of the most important training adaptations is an increase in the maximal oxygen uptake, called VO2 Max, which is a quantitative measure of a person's capacity for aerobic energy transfer (the ability to do work).

■ Variables that determine VO2 Max are heredity, sex, body composition (the amount of lean body tissue), age, and *training*.

■ Cardiovascular endurance comes first, then muscular endurance, followed by the connective tissues, tendons, and ligaments.

These are only samples of the knowledge a marathoner needs to reach his goal. One of the best ways to obtain this knowledge and receive the necessary physical training is to enter the Portland Marathon Training Clinics. Designed specifically for the Portland Marathon and organized by Patti and Warren Finke and Bob Williams, the training clinics prepare the virgin marathoner and sharpen the seasoned one.

The clinics are designed around proven training techniques for runners and walkers. These involve running

seconds. Deborah Raunig ran 2:43:51 on the Memorial Coliseum course. Lori Jorgensen ran a 2:43:21 on the downtown course.

■No pain, no gain.

Approximately 80% of the members of the Portland Marathon Training Clinics who run on Portland's steep and demanding Wildwood Trails

with clinic groups every other weekend, starting in March and lasting through the Marathon. They include seminars which teach them everything from finding the right pair of shoes to carbo-loading the week before the run. They familiarize runners and walkers with terms like electrolytes, hydration, and stress-fracture. Members of the training clinics (which become a large extended family) learn what the terms mean and how to cope with the changes and stresses their bodies are experiencing during their rigorous marathon training. Simultaneously, they develop a large respect for the Finkes and Bob Williams.

Runners enrolled in Portland Marathon Training Clinics experience the challenge of Wildwood Trails.

Patti Finke, exercise physiologist, and Warren Finke, computer nut, the owner-operators of wY'east Consulting (a consulting firm for the athlete) are both ultramarathoners. They run marathons as training runs for ultramarathons, which are normally forty to fifty miles long. Bob Williams, a well-known Masters coach with an M.S. in sports techniques, is a past Olympic qualifier (1972) and a friend of the Finkes. They approached Les Smith about forming a training clinic. Smith and the Marathon Committee thought it was an excellent idea, and the Portland Marathon Training Clinics took off, welcoming hundreds of runners and guiding them toward their marathon goal. In 1986, the Finkes authored and published *Marathoning: Start to Finish*, which is sold nationally and is an invaluable reference for any runner. The Finkes also developed a pace chart specifically for the Portland course. See page 84.

achieve personal records come race day. Those who choose to avoid the wooded trails, nested deep within Forest Park, finish but without the satisfaction of a P.R.

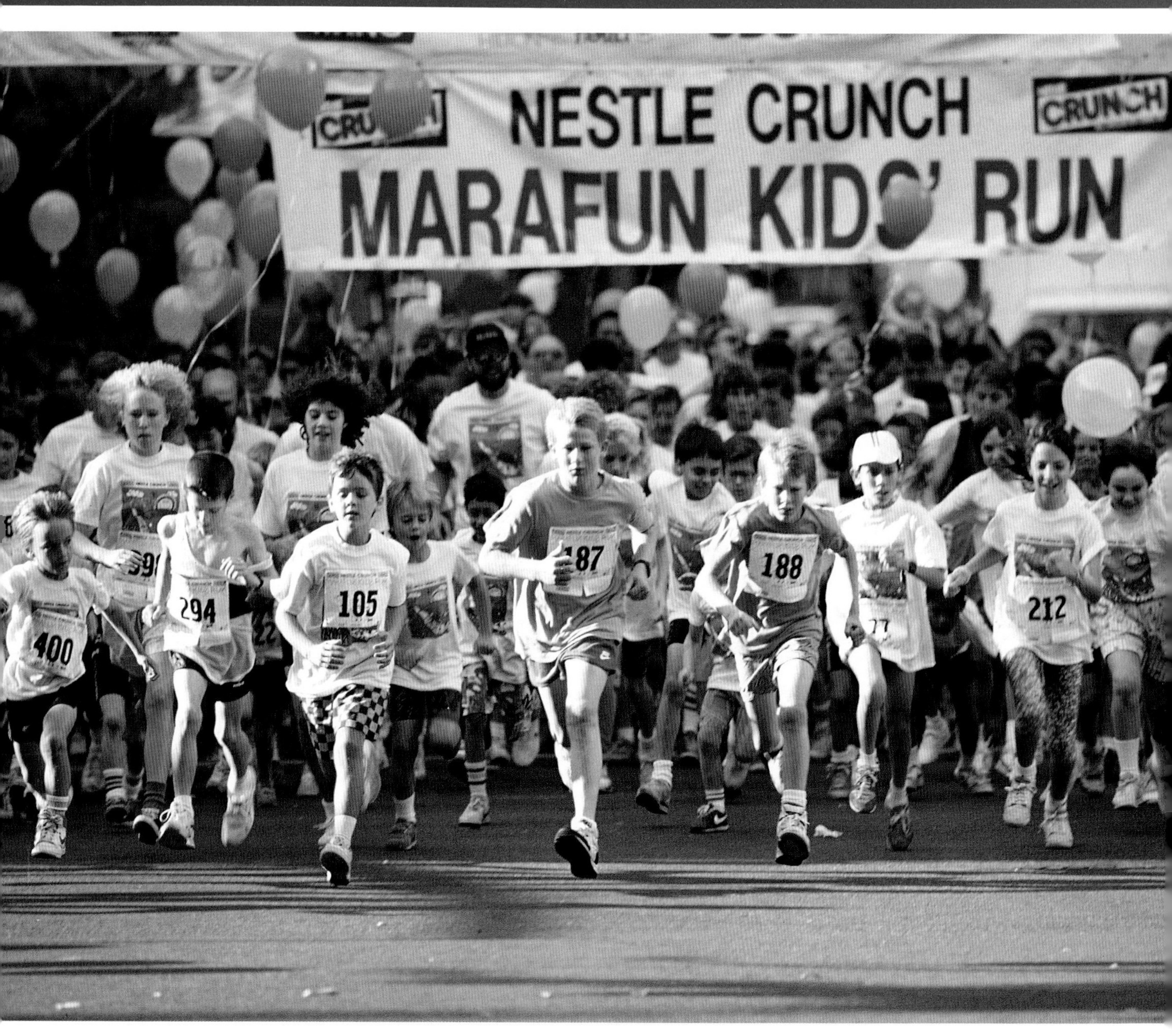
CRUNCH
NESTLE CRUNCH
CRUNCH
MARAFUN KIDS' RUN

RUNAWAY SUCCESS

Portland Marathon Events

> *"The real winners in this race were the runners who followed the leaders."*
>
> *Northwest Runner*

THE EVENTS

Thousands of runners and walkers participate in a multitude of rich and overlapping events.

The Wheelchair Marathon

The wheelchair athletes roll out just one minute prior to the 8:00 A.M. Marathon start. The magazine for wheelchair sport and recreation, *Sports 'N Spokes*, says, "Where there is a Wheel, there is a Way." This statement summarizes the determination of wheelchair athletes. Nothing can stop them.

One common aspect shared by all marathoners (runners, fast walkers, wheelchair competitors) is a certain look in the eye. It's a look that says "I'm going to do a marathon. I'm going to go the distance." Wheelchair athletes, like most marathon runners, don't necessarily listen to their doctors when they are told to take it easy, to stop training while an injury heals. They push their bodies to the limit. They start the Marathon at a quick 15 to 16 mph if they are in the lead. If they are in the middle of the pack, they will average about 12 to 13 mph. Traveling much faster than the runners, they seldom share the streets with the 4,000 marathoners who start behind them.

The race works at the wheelchair athlete's body. The circular motion of his forearms wears the muscles through to his shoulders. He is sweating under his helmet but he cannot waste the time stopping to wipe away moisture for fear of losing precious seconds. He tries to ignore his back when it yelps of discomfort. For the next few hours he is one with his chair, rolling with the course and fighting the wind.

A wheelchair marathoner does not casually own a racing chair, just as a runner does not casually own a pair of running shoes. He becomes schooled in aerodynamics, the best gloves on the market, and how to most effectively tape his hands. He knows how many miles his tires will take, just as the runner knows how many miles to put on his shoes before getting new ones. He often wishes there were shocks on racing

■The Portland Police are out in force during the Marathon, guarding the intersections, protecting crowds, and cheering on runners.

■Every year, volunteers

paint all the race and walk lines, hand out T-shirts and visors, and encourage kids to attend the Marafun. One year, they mistakenly painted

Ample protection for the hands can make or break a wheelchair athlete's finish time.

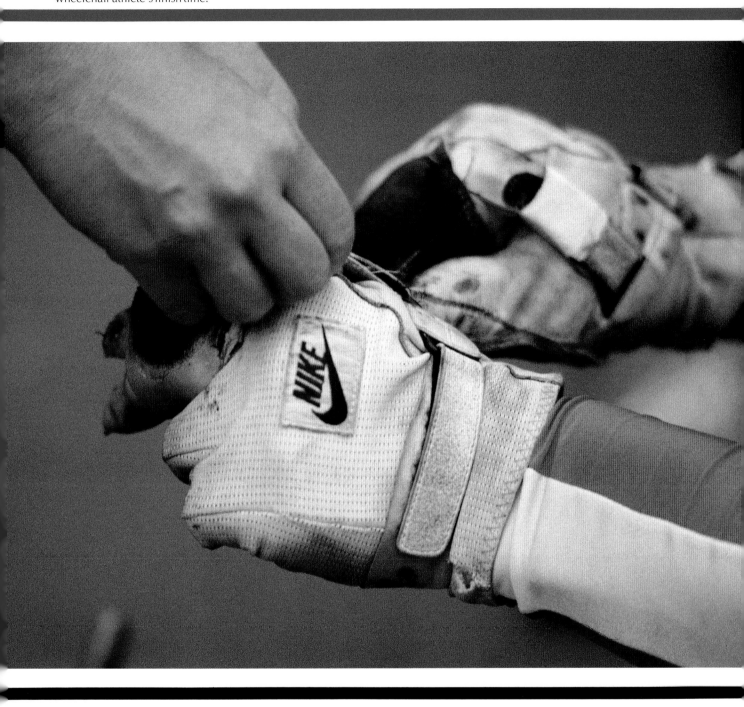

part of a line with non-washable paint. Another year, an irate resident, thinking that vandalism was afoot, hosed the paint off the street. There are lots of

line fiasco stories: pink paint, black paint, malfunctioning paint machines, you name it. Putting down lines is a demanding business.

■To keep tabs on the race, communications director Steve Crouch has ham-radio equipped cyclists following the front runners. In 1989, Larry Hinton was tracking the lead

Competitors eye each other's equipment and exchange the latest tips on wheelchair aerodynamics.

wheelchairs to lessen the bumpy ride, but he knows additions like that would cause the chair to become too heavy and ruin his time. He knows his chair inside and out.

The governing bodies of wheelchair athletes, the National Wheelchair Association (NWA) and the International Wheelchair Road Racing Association (IWRRA) are very specific about what courses and what wheelchairs qualify within their sports. (The Portland Marathon course is certified by TAC and therefore approved by both governing bodies for the Marathon course and the Five-Miler.)

It is thanks to Portland Marathon Committee members Jim Harding (OPVA representative) and Pat Holly (wheelchair athlete and Portland Marathon competitor since 1980) that the Portland Marathon offers a first class Wheelchair Marathon and Five-Mile event. It is Portland's local OPVA (Oregon Paralyzed Veterans Association) that worked to get Portland's course recognized by these two governing bodies as a premier wheelchair race. It was also the OPVA that made it possible for Portland's Wheelchair Marathon to offer prize money.

Although the Portland Marathon offers no prize money or appearance fees, the Oregon Paralyzed Veterans Association gives prize money to Marathon and Five-Mile finishers by sex and age group. It offers a bonus to the fastest time at the Marathon's half-way point and extra bonus money for breaking a course record. It includes a Quad Division and a Power Chair Division for those men and women who have limited

woman. He pedaled furiously, was knocked out by a flat tire, performed a desperate patch job, and spent the rest of the race trying to catch up.

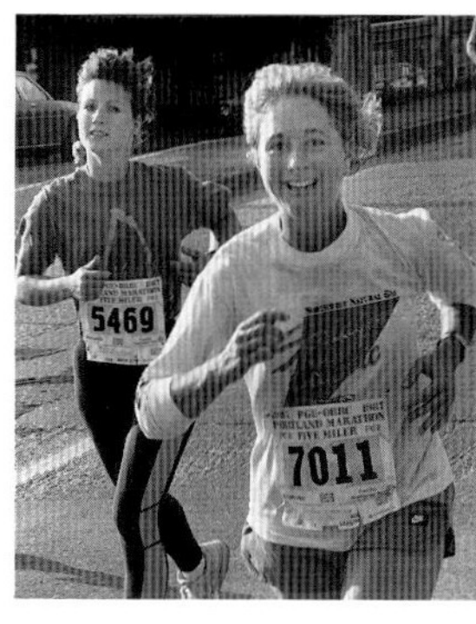

■Runners with a majority of slow twitch muscles may have to abandon hope of a fast finishing kick. Fast twitch muscles give winning times, but slow twitch muscles, which are fat burners, may make the difference between finishing and not finishing at all.

■Dr. George Sheehan

The 26.2 Mile Walk may sound like a snap, but it's no easy, early morning stroll.

use of their forearms and hands.

The Walks

The 1980s saw a surge of interest in the walker. This is a group respected by runners for their tenacity. Walkers include injured runners, burned-out runners, people who always wanted to run but for one reason or another could not, and people who never cared to run but just wanted to walk. It takes a walker perhaps twice the time as an average runner to complete the same distance, but complete it he or she does. Race-walkers have held the record for crossing the United States by foot.

The 26.2 Mile Marathon Walk

In 1989, the Portland Marathon Committee took a gamble and created the 26.2 Mile Marathon Walk. Portland has always had a special division for race-walkers, but this brand new event answered the need for a *noncompetitive* marathon walk.

A good measuring stick for the suc-

cess of this walk is the number of participants who registered in its first year, despite the 6 A.M. starting time. The Marathon Committee had planned for one hundred entrants but, when registration finally closed, the total count was over five hundred.

Improvisation seemed to be the key to that first year's success. Despite the unexpected turn-out, there were nearly enough Finisher's shirts, and Marathon medals were modified with special ribbons for walkers.

In its first year, the 26.2 Mile Walk

says, "The runner's world is divided into two worlds: the world of hills and the world of the flats." For training, Portland provides the world of the hills.

Stepping out for the Mayor's Walk.

followed the same course as the 26.2 Marathon. But in an effort to avoid traffic hazards associated with its early start, the Marathon Committee altered the front portion of the walk to avoid street crossings. Now walkers follow the Willamette River to Willamette Park near St. John's Landing and then link up with the course in Northwest, traveling the sidewalks rather than the streets, which are yielded to runners. The first year, some of the slower marathon walkers almost collided with those surging forward in the Mayor's Walk, but, these drawbacks aside, the Marathon Walk was deemed a smashing success and eligible for future repeats.

These initial walkers reported the kinds of feelings familiar to marathon runners. "It was a camaraderie like I experienced in boot camp." "It was a bonding with people I will never again experience." "We laughed and cried together all the way."

The Five-Mile Mayor's Walk

The Portland Marathon developed a marathon-related walking event, the first walk of its type in Portland, in 1986. Known officially as the Five-Mile Mayor's Walk, this event epitomized another of the Committee's mottos for the Marathon: "A Family Affair." It gave walkers the opportunity to participate along the same course that their family and friends were running.

With the launching of the Mayor's Walk, Portland's own Mayor actually participated in the Portland Marathon. Although he had been active with the Marathon in previous years, serving as a photographer since 1981, he had not

"Running the hills," Sheehan adds, "is for those of morbid mind who see and accept the evil in the world."

■**Former race director Ken Weidkamp says, "Marathon runners, like good wine, get better with age." In what may be a contradiction, Weidkamp also says, "The marathon keeps a**

actually participated. In 1986, Mayor Bud Clark established a tradition by walking the Mayor's Walk. Adding a personal but practical touch, he made the Mayor's Walk unique by walking the five miles in reverse.

Beginning downtown at the finish line, his Honor walks to Jefferson High School, where everyone else begins at 9 A.M. On his walk he snaps pictures of oncoming walkers and marathon runners in a tradition unparalleled in Marathon history.

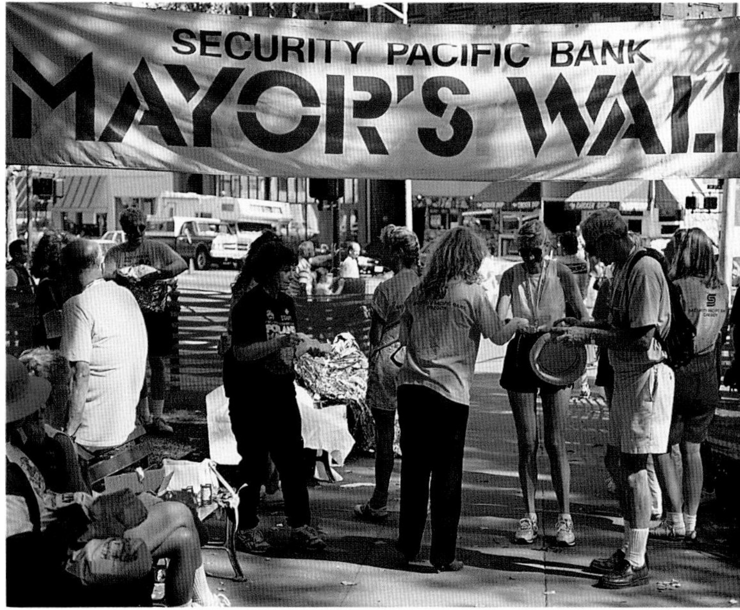

The Five-Mile Mayor's Walk reaches home base.

The Early Start Marathon

The Early Start Marathon, a new event created on demand by a serious group of slower athletes in 1988, is sometimes called the slow marathon. That, however, is not the best description of the early morning start, or the early morning starters. A more accurate description of the starters at this event, who begin their race one hour early, would be *determined.*

The Early Start was created for runners with estimated finish times of five hours or more. Heading off at dawn, these marathoners will run the race and complete it with the majority of the runners, who cross the finish line inside four hours. Early Starters get the thrill of finishing when the crowds are fresh and full of excitement, instead of coming to the end of their journey to find an abandoned finish area and no one to witness and applaud the end of their trying ordeal.

These early marathoners share not just the same course with the runners but also the same aid stations, volun-

person young for the rest of his life."

■Yoga stretching, massage, and swimming have, for years, been recommended for runners. Now, weight

With a blur of speed, the Early Start Marathoners take off in the dark.

training sessions are becoming part of a marathon training program. Runners have always consulted with a range of medical personnel to support their training programs, including doctors, podiatrists, chiropractors, orthopedic specialists, and acupuncturists, most of whom are also

teers, entertainment, energy, and enthusiasm. They have the same experiences that their faster counterparts do. They feel themselves go out at too fast a pace, calm down within the first five miles as their adrenalin finally settles, wonder at mile 9 why they have decided to run another marathon, or why they decided to run this one, their first. At the 10-mile mark, they begin to think seriously about what lies ahead. Will they hit the wall between 18 and 20 miles, will their legs, knees, arches hold out? They do a body check. At mile 15 they're looking for water, keeping an eye out for the aid stations.

The lead runners race past them at about mile 10. The bulk of the 8:00 A.M. runners pass them within the next four miles, but the early starters know it's okay, they just have to keep going. Mile 20. Hurrah! If they can just gut out the last 10K, they will pick up the prestigious Finisher's shirt and medal and be able to collapse in the park with everyone else.

Some of these Early Starters are well-known Masters marathoners. A famous Master who takes advantage of the early start is Mavis Lindgren, who lives in Orleans, California. Mavis started running marathons when she was fifty years old and now boasts of completing more than fifty. The early start gives her the time she needs to finish her run.

Pregnant women, injured runners who must slow their pace or not compete at all, older athletes, and younger competitors unsure of their finish times participate in the Early Marathon. One young woman, who prefers to remain anonymous, wrote to the Race Committee to thank them for the opportunity to begin the race early. She explained that she had been competing in marathons since her twenty-sixth birthday and had enjoyed finish times around the 3:45 mark. (Her best time was 3:36:06.) But over the course of the last several years, her times had drastically diminished. She had become clumsy, her right hip was often weak, and her energy for training seemed to have permanently gone South. Finally, after numerous tests her doctors diagnosed her with Multiple Sclerosis.

runners.

■**Thinking caffeine might help, as well as the fluid itself, a runner drank two sugary sodas half an hour prior to running**

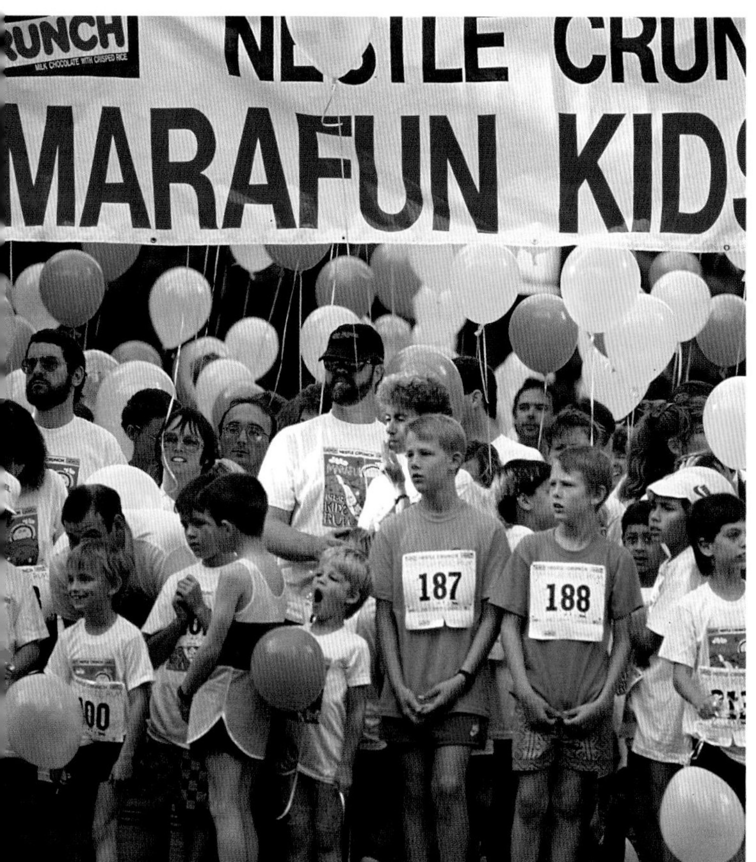

The Marafun brings big feet and small feet together.

It was on this note that the tone of her letter changed. She was thankful that her doctor was a runner and prescribed a moderate approach to running (when she had the energy) and even more thankful that the Race Committee offered an event that allowed her to run at her pace and not be embarrassed. "It's not the time that's hard on the ego," she wrote. "I can accept that. It's finishing by yourself that has been hard. But now I don't have to finish alone, or start alone, and when I look around the crowd I am racing with, I am proud. I count my blessings that I can still run and I include the Portland Marathon in my blessings for giving me and everyone else this opportunity to start early and finish with the crowds. Thank you, you've really made everyone a winner."

The Two-Mile Marafun

In keeping with its goal of making the Marathon a family affair, the Marathon Race Committee created an event just for kids in 1987. Kids twelve and under, that is, and their chaperones. At 9:10 A.M. on race day, a mass of giggling, energetic children, many wearing their event shirts all the way down to their ankles, accumulate for their own two-mile, noncompetitive event.

The gun fires, and they're off. The

the Marathon. Three miles into the race, he was overcome by exhaustion and was told by a doctor he should stop. He drank replacement fluids,

rested, and eventually finished the race in good time, learning later that he had probably experienced a hypoglycemia attack.

■The great fear of every

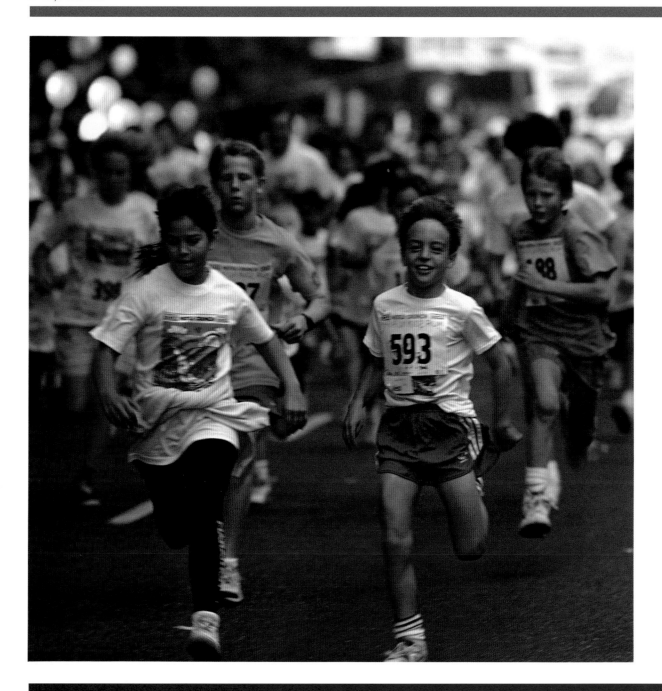

runner is arriving at the race after the starting gun has fired. Runners have confided this is a recurring nightmare.

■**The first lesson to be learned at a Portland**

Marathon Training Clinic is "No new is good new." In other words, never try anything new or different just before the Marathon. Stick to

Starting the race one minute ahead of runners, wheelchair athletes run with their arms.

bigger, more serious kids in the front of the pack are racing with pounding hearts, red faces. You can hear the pitter-patter of their swift feet. Children try to keep up with parents, grandparents, babysitters; parents, grandparents, and babysitters try to keep up with the kids, and everyone seems to be having a good time.

It's usually over within 30 or 45 minutes, depending on the pace. Some of the racers finish in 15 minutes. Some of the others, who have chosen to walk or skip or just plain dilly-dally, as children will, take longer. But with the exuberance earned by morning exercise and fresh air, they all eventually make it to the finish chute. With smiles on their faces and appetites demanding attention, they are rewarded with juice, water, munchies, and fruit.

They are satisfied. They have completed their distance. They have been part of the day's colorful festivities and they can go home with their own stories of unparalelled success and accomplishment. Christmas is for kids and so is the Marafun Kids' Run.

The Five-Miler

In 1985, in response to what the Race Committee deemed a marathon deficiency, the Marathon instigated its first satellite event. The Race Committee was seeing a large number of racers in the area, who, though not physically ready or interested in a 26.2-mile run, were interested in being a part of the

the clothes and foods you know.

■Rafael Ibarra, 1988 Wheelchair Marathon winner, took the wheelchair division in Honolulu, then came back to Portland in 1989 to set a course record time of 1:54:06.

■In 1988, due to a misunderstanding at the start line, the wheelchair athletes

Marathon. The question confronting the Committee was what to do about it.

The answer was the Five-Miler. It was felt that runners shy of the marathon would enjoy a shorter event which raced over the first part of the course while the marathon was underway. The response was tremendous that first year, and participation has increased each year since. The event, which speeds off at 8:30 A.M., is now the largest of its distance in the entire Northwest and draws more women (49 percent), a larger percentage than any comparable event in the nation.

Five-Mile finishing times are fast and competitive, as fast as 24:08 for men and 27:32 for women. Although these runners don't endure the mileage of the marathoner, they still experience the elation of a good morning's run, knowing they have done their best.

EVENTS WITHIN THE EVENTS

The Portland Marathon has added challenges within challenges for its entrants (and sometimes staggered its bookkeeping and computer timing staffs). Recognizing a need and fulfilling it is an important Race Committee goal.

When Committee members recognized they could incorporate team events in the Marathon and the Five-Miler and have more people participating as a result, they did not hesitate to find a way to do it. The Team Event alone has four subcategories, and there are ten more major events within the Marathon and the Five-Miler: Race-Walkers, Special Olympic Categories, Handicapped Runners Without Wheelchairs, the Stroller Event, Age Division Awards, Masters, State and Country Awards, the Clydesdale Event, and the Muscle Mania Division. All of these events have subcategories, and all these subcategories have awards. This might cause headaches at the finish line for the timing staff, but with good organization and impeccable volunteers it works.

Team Events

Team events for the Marathon and the Five-Miler fall into four categories:

were sent out ten minutes in front of the 8:00 A.M. pack instead of one minute. This caused problems when whizzing wheelchair athletes met runners head on at Marathon Avenue.

■For two consecutive years, the person wheeling second in the Marathon became so excited that he failed to

Corporate, Open, Masters, and Family. With the exception of the Family category, teams can number up to five members. However, only the scores of the top three team members are counted. Teams may be all male, all female, or co-ed. Of the three members of a co-ed team who score, at least one man or one woman must be counted.

Corporate Teams must hail from a corporation, business, or government agency. Nearly eighty teams from all over the Northwest participate in this category each year. There are no age divisions within the Corporate category, and team competition is spirited. Although members of a team may not be able to tell who they are competing against (they don't necessarily wear matching corporate shirts or any distinguishable labels), they race against each other to assure an excellent score. One triumphant team from Washington State University got so caught up in the competition, it created and dedicated a permanent corporate trophy, to be passed on year after year.

The Open category naturally welcomes all running clubs, athletic clubs, neighborhood and church groups, eating clubs, sporting teams, political groups, bowling teams, indeed any group, formal or informal, inclined to run as a team. Again, there must be five members on the team, which may be male, female, or co-ed. The same rules apply to Open as apply to Corporate teams. Likewise, competition is keen. When it's all over, the Marathon Committee is pleased to duplicate for those in the Open all of the awards given out in the Corporate category.

The Masters category is open to all runners over forty years old and is scored just the way Corporate and Open are. Because scores are based in part on a person's place within an age division, Masters competition is attractive regardless of how old a competitor may be.

The Family team event is a source of enthusiastic competition. A family team can consist of any combination or the whole fam-damily. Both members of two-person family teams score. In larger family teams, the top three are counted.

negotiate the turn down Lovejoy ramp and headed back into the Northwest section of town.

■**A very special athlete from Canada who has**

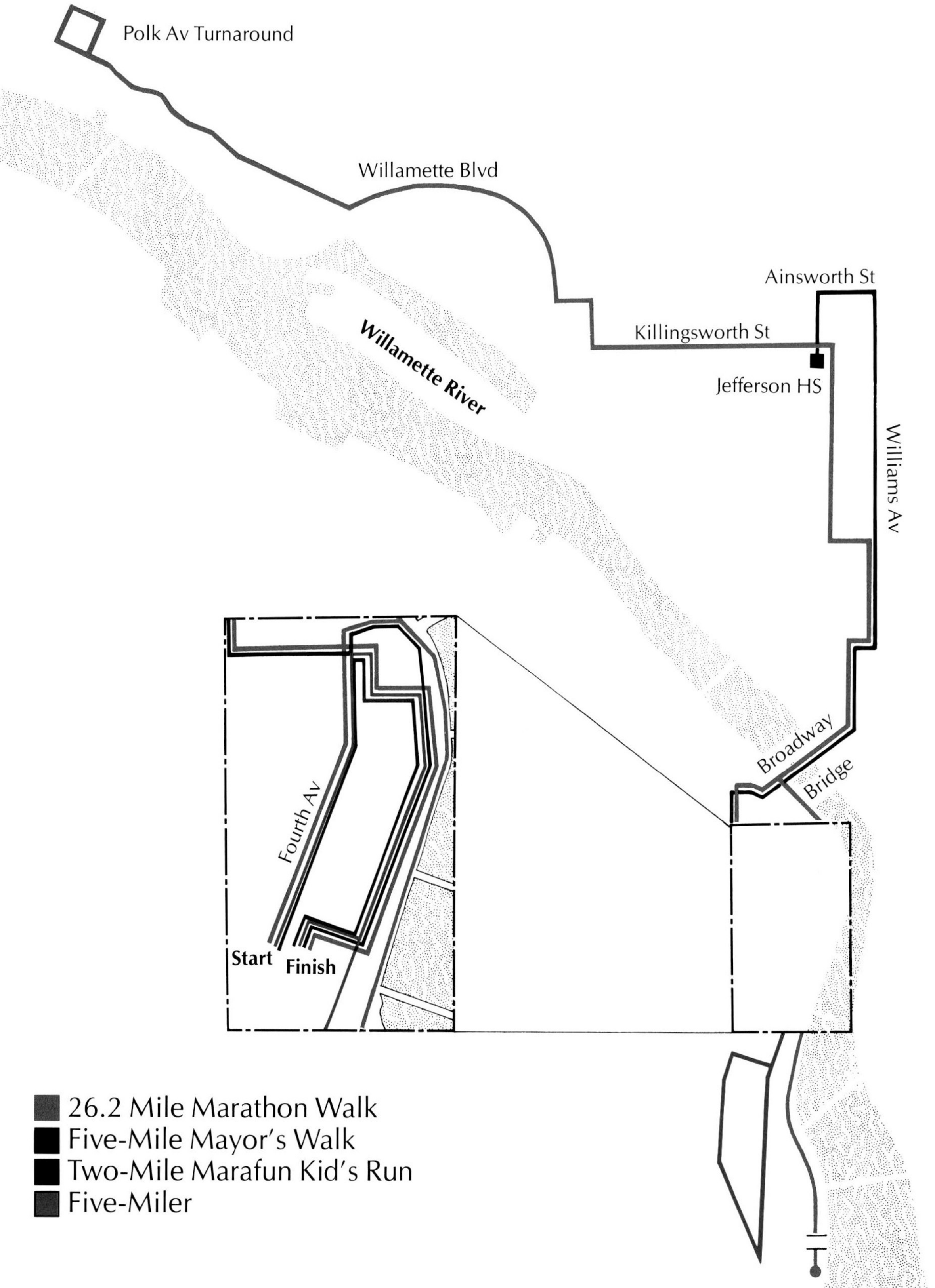

26.2 Mile Marathon Walk
Five-Mile Mayor's Walk
Two-Mile Marafun Kid's Run
Five-Miler

A runner dares the distance with the help of his cane and young daughter.

Even nuclear and extended families participate.

Race Walkers

The first thing to be said of the Race Walkers is that they are not casual walkers. The pace set by the Race Walker is often the same as that set by the marathoner. The word *walk* in Race Walker does not imply slow, and the fact that Portland Marathon Race Walkers have completed the 26.2 miles between 3:15 and 5:00 hours is testament to their ability to hold their own.

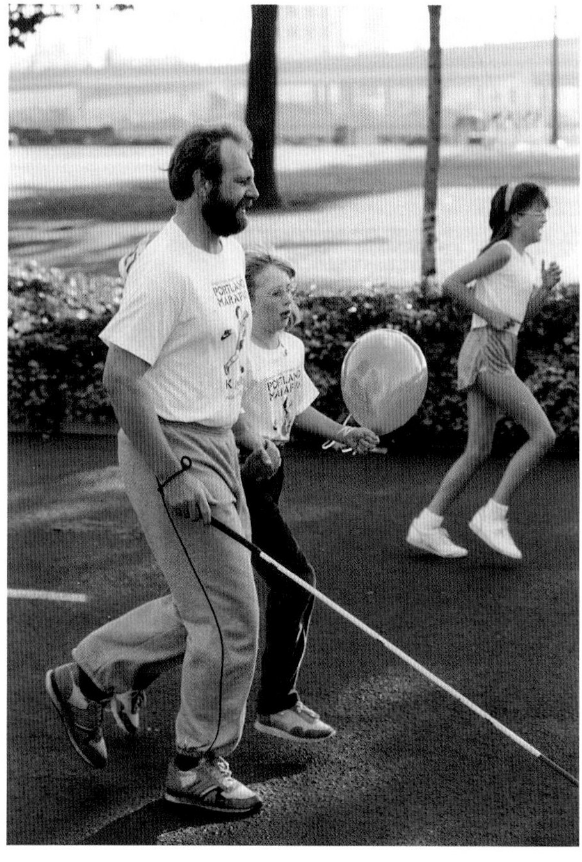

Race Walkers participate in both the Portland Marathon and the Five-Miler. They do not compete in the 26.2-Mile Walk or in the Five-Mile Mayor's Walk because these are nontimed events.

The fluid, arm-swinging, pelvis-gyrating rhythm that Race Walkers attain is a foreign motion to most marathoners. But runners admire their tenacity in maintaining the motion throughout the distance, and secretly, many may be glad they are running, not fast walking. To them, race walkers look as if they are working much harder.

Special Olympic Categories

A long-standing category in both the Marathon and Five-Miler allows Special Olympics athletes to compete. No group of runners tries harder to go the distance. Many train by running with

a congenitally weakened leg uses a crutch to help him run the Marathon. Each year, he has finished in the respectable time of 3:30.

A small blue bundle awaits the back-of-the-pack stroller start with parents who interpret "a family affair" literally.

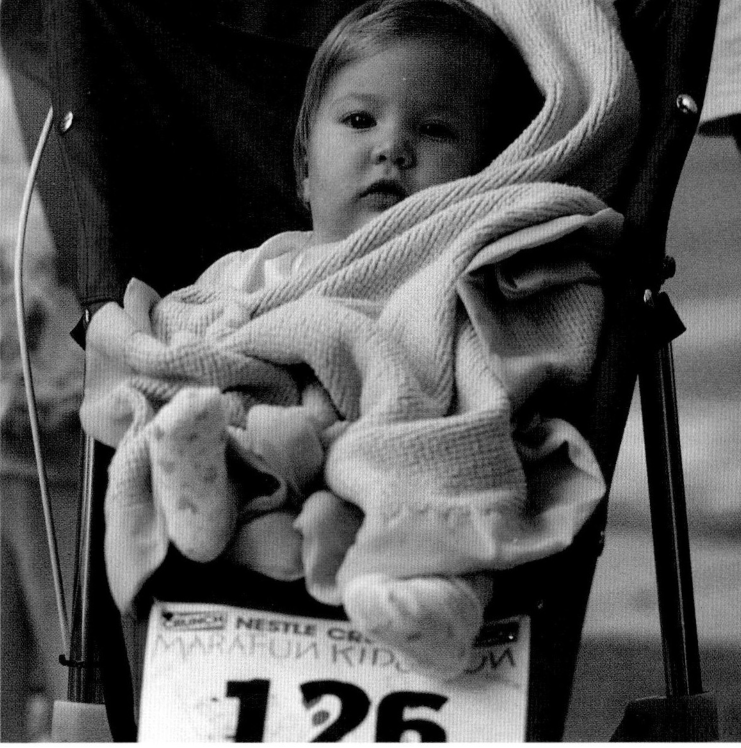

Portland Marathon Training Clinics. The Marathon's efforts to assist this dedicated cadre of athletes is aimed at creating a magnet program that will attract Special Olympics athletes from chapters all over the United States.

Handicapped Runners Without Wheelchairs

The event for handicapped runners without wheelchairs means exactly what it says. Anyone with a handicap not requiring a wheelchair may participate in this category by mailing in, with his registration form, a letter explaining his handicap. As a result, blind runners, deaf runners, amputees with and without a prosthesis, and runners on crutches have participated. Past marathons have seen both men and women without legs competing on skateboards.

These runners are warmly encouraged by crowds and fellow athletes. Acknowledgment awards are given to each and every one of them. They are not given awards based on their finish times, although many place in regular age division categories. They are given awards based on overcoming a handicap and completing the distance, be it the Marathon distance, the Five-Miler, the Marathon Walk, the Five-Mile Walk, or the Kids' Marafun.

The Stroller Event

Almost everyone has driven by some man or woman sweating along the road

■At about 17 miles, a runner took a drink from one of the volunteers, ran on, rounded the turnaround and came back to the same aid station for

and pushing a stroller full of a bundle of joy weighing up to forty pounds. It seemed harmless when those with strollers started entering, but as their numbers grew, race officials realized there were potential dangers involved. At the same time, TAC and the Road Runners Club of America (RRCA) began discouraging race officials from allowing stroller-pushers in their races. While the Portland Marathon Committee recognized the difficulties, it believed strollers could be safely handled.

The Race Committee decided that many problems could be overcome by starting the stroller participants at the back of the pack. In fact, a stroller is no more dangerous in a race than a wheelchair, and the Marathon Committee has made bookends of the wheeled apparatuses allowed on race day. The wheelchairs start one minute prior to the start of the marathon; the strollers start about one minute after the last runners cross the starting line.

There are no age group divisions in the Stroller Event, no handicap offered for the weight of the baby, and no weight or sex division for the pusher. For the men and women who have found that the only way they can train is by taking their child with them, this is an arduous but apparently satisfying way to spend a Sunday morning. Their pleasure is heightened when they pass peers without strollers.

Forty and Under

The triumph of Five-Milers and Marathoners crossing their respective finish lines is heightened when plaques and trophies are presented at the Post-Race Party and Awards Ceremony.

Beautiful brass and Oregon hardwood plaques are given to the top fifteen finishers, beginning with age twenty in the Marathon and age fourteen in the Five-Miler. The awards, which divide men and women into separate categories, are presented to winners in five-year increments until age forty. Thereafter, awards are given to men and women in five-year increments, with special acknowledgment for the achievements of Masters.

more water. The same volunteer asked him how he was doing. When the runner said he could use a partner, the volunteer ran the next couple of miles

with him. Once she knew he was alright, she stopped at another aid station to help out, and the thankful runner headed toward the finish line.

Masters

Masters participating in the Portland Marathon are forty years and over. In 1915, the Amateur Athletic Union (AAU) created the Masters Division in track and field events. The age of forty was established as the Rubicon separating Masters and nonMasters. Since its inception in 1972, the Portland Marathon has offered a Masters Division. When the Five-Miler came into existence in 1985, it followed suit.

Do not let age fool you. Just because a runner is over forty does not mean he is going to race with the Early Start Marathon. Nor does it mean his time will be slow. At age sixty-five, at the Portland Marathon, Clive Davies set a World Masters Marathon Record of 2:42:22, a time that many a younger athlete will strive to attain, and never reach, in a lifetime.

Country and State Awards

The Portland Marathon acknowledges entrants from every state in the Union and from every foreign country. A first place award is given to the male and female marathon winners of each state and nation. Consequently, runners and walkers compete against members of their own sex and against members of

■**Bryan Clemen, who has both legs amputated at the knees, rolled across the finish line of the 1983 Marathon in 2:38:23, just 21 minutes behind**

their state or country. First place awards also go to Five-Mile finishers. Each year, citizens from as many as forty-eight states and fourteen foreign countries enter the Portland Marathon.

Runners from Oregon and Washington are part of still another competition. Winners in both male and female categories compete to be named best Northwest runner, and Oregon offers two other awards to the fastest male and female in the greater Portland metropolitan area. As can be imagined, these awards create a lot of fierce, local competition.

Clydesdales

The Clydesdale Event is the Portland Marathon's "large runner" event. Clydesdales are a breed of fine draft horses. Referring to the immensity of these horses and their ability to do a hard day's work, a group of big runners began calling themselves the Clydesdale Association and lobbied for equality where running and weight were concerned. Their desires were met, and the Portland Marathon has offered a big runner category for men since 1984 and for women since 1987.

Clydesdales include men and women with larger physiques than the typical svelte running shape. Weight classifications for men begin at 185 pounds. Weight classifications for women begin at 155 pounds. These subcategories are further divided between runners over-forty (Masters) and under forty (non-Masters). Those competing are weighed in on doctor's scales set up at the Fitness Fair and in front of the Portland Building on Sunday morning. Their weight is fed into the Marathon computer so when they cross the finish line the results of the competition are known at once.

Muscle Division

The Muscle Marathon or the Muscle Division of the Marathon brings a whole new meaning to the term "cross training." It is a small and interesting event that began as an experiment. Many men and women body builders enjoy running

Monte Brothwell's winning time. Clemen pushed himself along on his hands, which are protected with gloves, pulled himself forward inch by inch

Legs of steel. After overpowering weight-plates, Ironmen conquer the Marathon.

on the hills and let his skateboard rip when he reached a downhill slope.

■The first Portland Marathon saw 98 finishers under the age of 19. The youngest competitor was 12-year-old Robert Arkes, Jr. The oldest runner was Joe Mallon, age 51. Only eight women ran.

■Running is reputed to

but they do not put in as many miles as they would like for fear they will burn too much muscle during long training runs. However, they want to run a marathon and they have the strength and endurance to go the distance, albeit probably not at a 5-or 6-minute pace.

The Muscle Division is based on how much weight a person can bench press and then still run 26.2 miles or five miles. A competition for both men and women, its awards are based on the weight bench-pressed in relationship to body weight and running time. It is an event for a Hercules who runs like Pheidippides.

OTHER EVENTS

Sports and Fitness Exposition

The Sports and Fitness Expo is a constant flow of people. Under a magnificent chandelier outside the ballroom, and reflecting in the floor-to-ceiling mirrors, runners move down toward the ballroom on escalators. Off the escalators, they immediately join one of the number of long lines to pick up their race number. Then they join friends and family to take advantage of a runner's dream—dozens of booths with products all aimed at them.

Athletic companies have the opportunity to show and sell their wares to a captive audience of nearly 20,000 enthusiastic and knowledgeable consumers. Runners pick up hard-to-find items like Gortex water-and-wind-resistant mittens and they find more common running apparel such as shorts and running shoes. One woman buys her coveted, blister-free socks at the Expo. "It's the only place I bother to look for them," she says. Cardiovascular assessments are available, and Nike uses computers to print out pace charts based on personal estimated marathon or five-mile finish times.

Like the Marathon, the Sports and Fitness Exposition culminates a year's work. The Marathon concludes a year's training and running, while the Sports and Fitness Expo celebrates that training and represents the end of a year of effort for the Portland Marathon Race

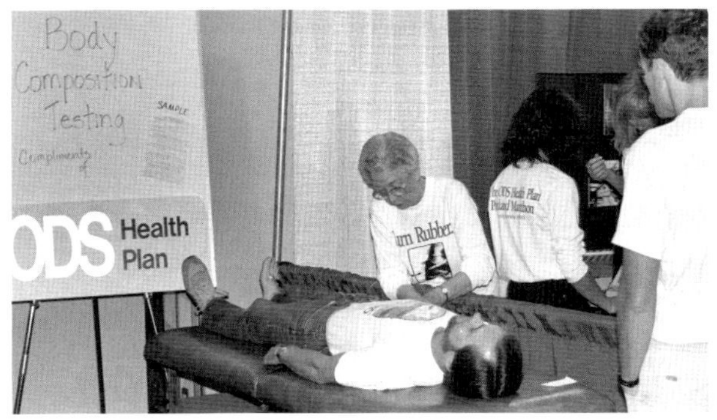

decrease the runner's chances of a heart attack by almost 45% and to increase the probability he'll be squashed by a truck by 600%. Cardiovascular

Committee. The Expo welcomes Marathon participants, readies them for the big day, provides them with needed registration paraphernalia, sells them Marathon souvenirs, and offers them toured bus rides of the Marathon course on Saturday.

The Expo used to be held in a small downtown sports store on the Saturday before the Marathon. Now it opens in the Hilton's huge ballroom on the Friday morning prior to the Marathon and closes Saturday evening. Winding their way through long lines, runners and walkers pick up their race packets which include their race number and safty pins, *Fanfare*, (the Marathon's pre-race magazine), and last minute instructions and maps. They also get a goody bag stuffed with sponsor products, including Vaseline, hand-lotion, heat rubs, restaurant coupons, candy-bars, and other items which the "bag stuffers" think may please the runners. Participants also pick up the much-in-demand event T-shirts (except for marathoners, who receive their T-shirt after they finish the race).

Runners are as nervous at the Expo as they are at the start line. They talk about their training and usually they downplay it. "Oh, I haven't really trained at all. I'm just going to show up and do the best I can." For some reason, a marathoner cannot admit he is running 80 to 100 miles a week and running six minutes per mile. He cannot admit he's been running well. He knows the distance he has to accomplish. But no matter how well trained a marathoner may be, he doesn't want to jinx himself.

The marathoner's attitude seems to infiltrate the other runners. Even Five-Milers are reluctant to talk about their

efficiency may improve by 100%, but the risk of being chewed by a dog increases by 700%.

■Each year, hundreds of volunteers set up entertainment and

aid stations. The only brawn strong enough to assemble the Marathon scaffolding at the start and finish lines is a local rugby team alliteratively named the

expected performance. All seem ready to claim they are not well-trained. Even walkers, who have had a steady diet of long distance work-outs on Portland's Wildwood Park trails and countless other historical hikes around town, claim they aren't trained yet. There is one exception. Nearly every child who registers at the last minute for the two-mile Marafun seems confident in his or her abilities to finish. Ironically, the fact is that almost everyone at the Expo will go the distance and many will make personal bests. Somehow, on Sunday, they will have what it takes to finish.

The Pasta Party and T-Shirt Swap

The evening before the Marathon, thousands of runners and walkers race toward an event dear to their stomachs. This is a special event, one that nurtures Marathon participants and benefits the causes dear to the Portland Marathon's heart. This is the Pasta Party and T-Shirt Swap.

Named for exactly what it is, a serving of pasta and a party of people there to eat it and trade nostalgia, the Pasta Party and T-Shirt Swap is the runner's last chance to receive needed carbohydrates. Although running magazines and sports physiologists tell athletes that they need to be carbo loading several days before the run, they still can use the additional carbohydrates from their last meal the night before the challenging Marathon.

Once inside, the T-Shirt Swap begins. The Swap offers unique shirts that, although already worn, are valued commodities to the runner. Swapping a shirt with a stranger may seem eccentric to some, but the lure of this event is great and makes the wait for dinner less aggravating.

When finally seated at the long rows of tables, runners and their families talk of the next day's great events. They discuss what time they will arrive at their start, how they feel, what they hope and what they dread. They show off their newly swapped T-shirts. They talk about the food, how wonderful it tastes, how they hope it helps. And, being the diet-conscious people that

Portland Pigs.

■About twelve key Portland Marathon Committee members labor all year long on the Marathon. Seventy Marathon Committee

A full belly and a new T-shirt—the little things that make runners happy.

members work six months out of the year, and several hundred volunteers help the week prior to the race. No less than 3,000 volunteers help to

Satisfied delight concludes the Pasta Party.

they are, they converse at length about the possible impact this carbohydrate party may have on their physique. (Runners are always concerned about calories and hope they are able to burn these calories off during their run.)

At one Pasta Party, a woman was overheard to say that she started marathoning to lose weight. "I figure I drop about 100 calories per mile, which is 2,600 calories on race day alone, disregarding training miles. I can eat almost anything!" Less lucky marathoners have been known to put on the pounds in the week prior to race day due to an uncontrolled splurge of carbo-loading.

One year, fifteen hundred runners lined up at Pasta Party tables only to discover that the lasagna had not arrived. The company supplying it from their restaurant about a mile away was held up when a crucial roadway was blocked by a police chase. Low-based rumbles grew to an impatient tapping of utensils on empty plates, accompanied by pounding silverware on metal tables. It was an overture of unhappy, growling stomachs until the lasagna arrived.

Charities work to organize the Party and benefit from it. Helping the charities to feed these hungry patrons are a number of businesses which make the event a happy success with donations of food and drinks.

The untroubled departure of the patrons is the antithesis of their arrival. They are full and satisfied and their nerves, for the moment, have been soothed. The Pasta Party and T-Shirt Swap is an event that gives families the chance to bond and fellow participants the opportunity to become comrades. One runner refers to his dinner as his last supper. He says that if he doesn't

make race day Sunday a success.

■In 1989, volunteers preparing registration materials at the Sports and Fitness Expo broke a packet-stuffing record by one full hour. Forty-nine staunch workers filled 10,934 race packets in three and a half hours.

■Over the years, members of the

make it through the Marathon he at least had a last good meal with his family and if he does make it through—the Pasta Party is something to look forward to next year.

Volunteer Phenomenon

Behind this great tidal action are thousands of humble heroes, the volunteers who make it all possible. From where do they all come? That is the question.

During the summer, as the Marathon draws near, Race Director Les Smith and the Marathon Committee get anxious. They begin to talk about what they call the "volunteer phenomenon" in hopes that it will happen again. While the Race Committee's Volunteer Coordinators are holding volunteer meetings and workshops, Les and the committee count heads. How many volunteer bodies are in attendance? Les counts them, counts them again, adds, multiplies, and is terrified there will not be enough bodies on the course come race day.

Then, Les remembers the phenomenon, the miracle. The Volunteer meetings collect about 30 percent of the volunteers, mostly new recruits. The other 70 percent are under the control of volunteer captains who keep in touch with their volunteers from previous years. These numbers miraculously swell when a sudden flood of unexpected friends and neighbors of regular volunteers show up Marathon morning to work

Northwest Four-Wheel Drive Association, the "mobile members," have served as a reconnaissance unit. Another key group of ham radio operators is

Everybody helps. A young, unofficial volunteer hands out sponges at a neighborhood aid station.

alongside their friends.

Les cannot explain it. He says, "It's a phenomenon! Somehow the volunteers always come. They seem to split and divide! They are a wonderful group of people. They work their tails off, and all they get is a T-shirt and a visor." (Over thirty-two hundred T-shirts and visors are passed out.)

On race day, hundreds of these volunteers will be hosing down runners, handing out food, providing entertainment and helping with finish results. Hundreds of others will have painted lines, set up viewing stands, helped at the Expo, raised thousands of dollars, and prepared publicity. Approximately one hundred and fifty volunteers will serve as medical aid assistants, including race course volunteers on bikes and a four-wheel drive brigade. Les Smith says, "Without the volunteers there would be no Portland Marathon. Afterwards we try to thank them all by sending them letters and our result book. Unfortunately, all these great volunteers do not register. Many go nameless, but not unappreciated."

housed in a mobile trailer at the finish line and handles another part of the Marathon's communication network.

■Two fixtures on the

Before the race, volunteers hammer down the red carpet of welcome at the finish area.

course are the Chicken Man and the Jammin' Salmon. Chicken Man, dressed in complete Big Bird costume, hoses down runners and supplies them with cups of water. Jammin' Salmon, dressed in scales, cheers runners on and, naturally, dispenses water.

ORRC
MARATHON
18TH ORRC
MARATHON
1989
FINISHER
WESTERN FAMILY

THE FINISH LINE

An Odyssey Ends

"The goal I can neither reach nor let go of is out there somewhere."

Joan Benoit
Olympic Champion

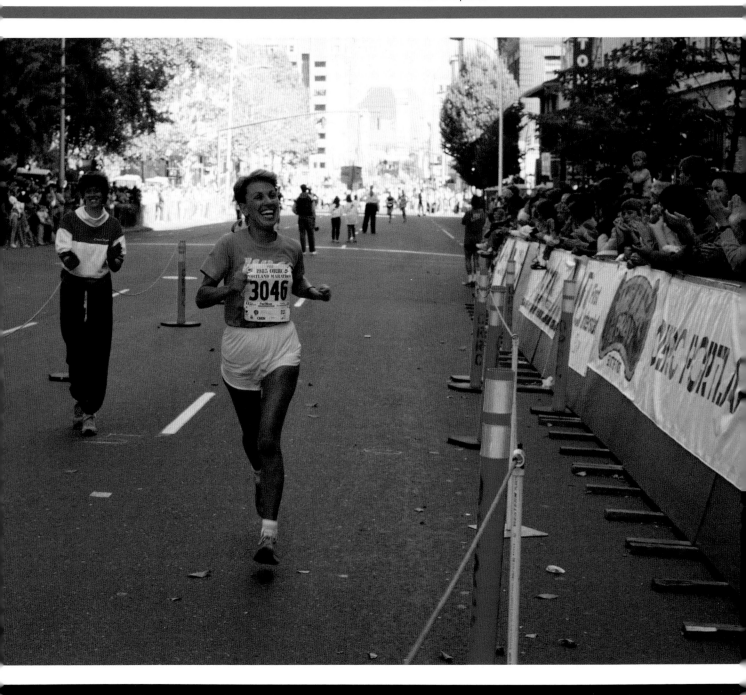

■"Just a short note to sincerely thank you for another excellent Portland Marathon," writes Bernard W. Reed of Portland, Oregon. "I am pleased to have

The finish line is hugs, pats on the back, laughter, and tears. It is an emotional time. Every finish is different. The finish line for children ends as it starts with their T-shirts around their knees and the sound of their cheerful voices. The finish line for Five-Mile runners is intense, the exhilarated end of a head-long sprint. The finish line for Five-Mile walkers is joyful and happy. Seldom is it confused with tears of laughter and cries of sorrow. The finish line for the 26.2-Mile walker is a quieter experience. The walker's journey has been difficult, even agonizing at times. When he receives a Finisher's shirt, he will wear it with pride.

For the marathoner, crossing the finish line is an ecstatic relief. He has lost five to ten pounds running. He has put his body through a pounding punishment. He is exhausted. His running shoes are permanently molded on his feet. He is in the grip of a powerful emotion. The marathoner crossing the finish line is laughing and crying and, often, collapsing.

For each marathoner, walker, five-miler, the finish line means something a little different; for each it is an utterly individual experience. But as his emotions quiet down, he begins to respond to his physical needs. Wrapped in a silver mylar blanket, a finish medal swinging around his neck, the mara-thoner finds liquid refreshment and food. He takes a nap in Lownsdale Park, if he's tired, gets assistance from the medical tent, if necessary. He may sign up for a massage. He is pampering a body that is still astonished it ran a total of 26.2 miles on a single Sunday morning in September.

After meeting his needs and check-

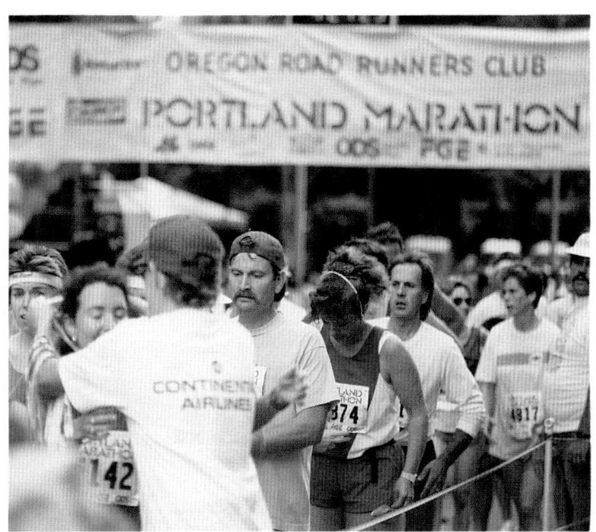

broken the world marathon record for a man 75 years and older. The only problem is my age is 40."

■**"Obviously at 3:11:00 we are not serious runners, but it is nice to know that we can test our own abilities, however limited, and still be treated like a winner," comment Darrel and**

Directly between the start and finish areas, the Portland Elk stands guard over finishers and spectators.

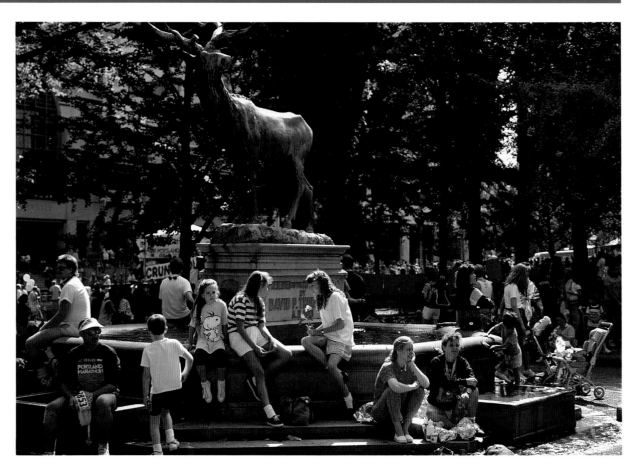

ing his time on the posted finish line print-out sheets, the marathoner goes to the Portland Building to pick up his coveted Finisher's shirt. Printed with the three Marathon colors chosen for that year, the shirt is emblazoned with the course directions and date. The runner will never forget what he did to get it. Later, he may attend the Post-Race Party where awards are given to all the different categories of Portland Marathon event winners and achievers. At the party, all the runners will relive their experiences with fellow marathoners, discuss the day, their times. Some will be satisfied with their performances;

Sharon Uriacher from Spokane, Washington. ■"This will be my third Portland Marathon and I keep returning because it is one of the best marathons I have run. Every runner is treated like they are the first runner over the finish line," applauds Anne McBride of Vancouver, British Columbia.

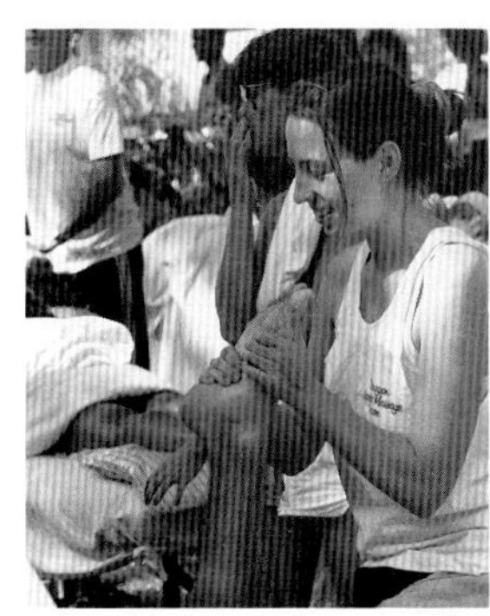

others, who did not run fast enough to meet their own impeccable standards, will be in the throes of despair. A few obsessed souls will be talking about their next marathon.

For everyone, the experience has been a passage, one they will recall when they are in bed that night and in the days to come. Another Portland Marathon has ended. Runners and walkers have headed for home. The deserted and littered streets have been cleaned by diligent crews. Les Smith and the Portland Marathon Committee are breathing a collective sigh of happy relief. *The Oregonian* and *Willamette Week* are preparing to print the voluminous record of race results.

Out of this Portland Marathon, out of the Marathons that have been and the Marathons to come, are stories of human courage and aspiration, stories of patience and perseverance, stories of generosity and hard work, laughter, and tears. The Portland Marathon has been an experience filled with both solitude and camaraderie, with challenges met and memories to be cherished.

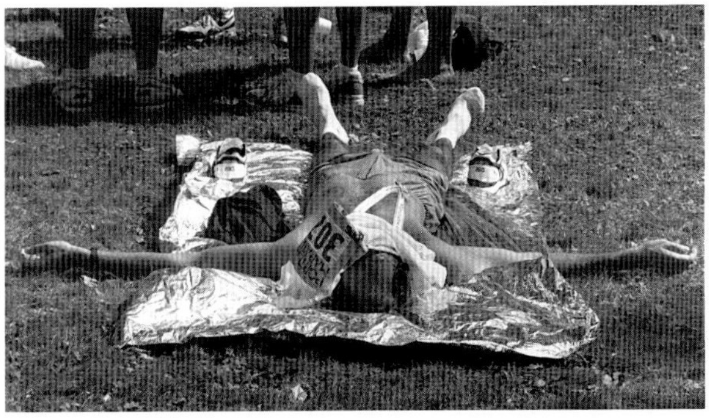

"It takes a special group to make torture fun and I hope you do it again," says Brian Steeley of Sisters, Oregon.

■"My only suggestion for improvement would be to move the wall to mile 27," writes Ken Koch of Brush Prairie, Washington.

Personal Marathon Record

Marathon: ______________________
Place: ______________________
Date: ____________
Finish Time: ____________
Overall Place: ____________
Age Group Place: ____________
Place by Sex: ____________
Pace/Mile: ____________
Goal: ____________
Race Conditions: ______________________

Your photo proof from the race

Marathon: ______________________
Place: ______________________
Date: ____________
Finish Time: ____________
Overall Place: ____________
Age Group Place: ____________
Place by Sex: ____________
Pace/Mile: ____________
Goal: ____________
Race Conditions: ______________________

Your photo proof from the race

Marathon: ______________________
Place: ______________________
Date: ____________
Finish Time: ____________
Overall Place: ____________
Age Group Place: ____________
Place by Sex: ____________
Pace/Mile: ____________
Goal: ____________
Race Conditions: ______________________

Your photo proof from the race

Marathon: ______________________
Place: ______________________
Date: ____________
Finish Time: ____________
Overall Place: ____________
Age Group Place: ____________
Place by Sex: ____________
Pace/Mile: ____________
Goal: ____________
Race Conditions: ______________________

Your photo proof from the race

Marathon: ______________________
Place: ______________________
Date: ____________
Finish Time: ____________
Overall Place: ____________
Age Group Place: ____________
Place by Sex: ____________
Pace/Mile: ____________
Goal: ____________
Race Conditions: ______________________

Your photo proof from the race

Marathon: ______________________
Place: ______________________
Date: ____________
Finish Time: ____________
Overall Place: ____________
Age Group Place: ____________
Place by Sex: ____________
Pace/Mile: ____________
Goal: ____________
Race Conditions: ______________________

Your photo proof from the race

Marathon: ______________________
Place: ______________________
Date: ____________
Finish Time: ____________
Overall Place: ____________
Age Group Place: ____________
Place by Sex: ____________
Pace/Mile: ____________
Goal: ____________
Race Conditions: ______________________

Your photo proof from the race

Marathon: ______________________
Place: ______________________
Date: ____________
Finish Time: ____________
Overall Place: ____________
Age Group Place: ____________
Place by Sex: ____________
Pace/Mile: ____________
Goal: ____________
Race Conditions: ______________________

Your photo proof from the race

AD RUNNER
D MARATHON!

Color Photo Credits

Bill Blanchard ■ 17A & D, 27, 59A, C, & D, 81, 116

Tony Capone ■ 17C, 45, 49, 59B, 63, 66, 93, 125

Bud Clark ■ 64, 94, 100, 104

Terry Crawford ■ 33B, 69, 80, 115, 122, 123

Kristin Finnegan ■ 3, 10-16, 21-24, 29-32, 33A, C, & D, 37-40, 48, 51-58, 60, 61, 65, 68, 70-78, 82-92, 95-99, 105-114, 117-121, 124, 128

The photo on page 127 by Kristin Finnegan in collaboration with Tony Capone.

Yukihiko Yamaoki ■ 17B, 79

Black and White Photo Credits

Tony Capone ■ Except as noted, all black and white photographs are by Tony.

Kristin Finnegan ■ 12B & D, 13A & C

Oregon Distance Runner ■ 34C, 36A & C, 37B & C, 38C & D, 39A & D, 40B, 57D, 60B & D

Pictures of the Portland Marathon from 1972-1987 were all lost due to water damage in storage.

Bibliography

Benoit, Joan and S. Baker. 1987. *Running Tide*. New York: Alfred A. Knopf.

Finke, Patti and Warren. 1986. *Marathoning: Start to Finish*. Portland, OR: wY'east Publishing.

Fixx, Jim. 1980. *Jim Fixx's Second Book of Running*. New York: Random House.

Galloway, Jeff. 1984. *Galloway's Book on Running*. Bolinas, CA: Shelter Publications, Inc.

Henderson, Joe. 1980. *The Running Revolution*. Eugene, OR: Gemini Books.

Hopkins, John. 1966. *The Marathon*. London: Stanley Paul & Company Ltd.

Lebow, Fred and R. Woodley. 1984. *Inside the World of Big-Time Marathoning*. New York: Rawson Associates.

Runner's World Magazine Editors. 1974. *The Boston Marathon*. Winter Park, FL: World Publications.

Runner's World Magazine Editors. 1978. *The Complete Runner*. New York: AvonBooks.

Ullyot, Dr. Joan. 1976. *Women's Running*. Winter Park, FL: World Publications.

N.B. *The Oregonian* covers the Marathon each year and is a valuable source of information; as is *Willamette Week*, which publishes finish results; *The Oregon Distance Runner*; *Sports 'N Spokes*; and *The New York Times*.

Running marathons has always been author Nadine Wooley's passion. She raced in fifteen marathons and twenty triathlons on the West Coast and in Hawaii, New York, and Europe before being slowed down by Multiple Sclerosis. Her favorite race is the Portland Marathon, and she has now written its definitive history, including all its colorful events.

Raised on a farm on the Southern Oregon Coast, a graduate of Whitman College, and a former wholesale lumber broker, Nadine lives in Portland with her husband, Marathon Race Director Les Smith, and their daughter, Ann Marie.